THE YIN AND YANG
OF ORGANIZATIONS

This book is to be returned on or before
the last date stamped below.

LONDON BOROUGH OF SUTTON
WALLINGTON LIBRARY
Shotfield, Wallington, Surrey SM6 0HY
081-770 4900

RENEWALS   *Please quote:* date of return, your ticket number
and computer label number for each item.

RENEWALS   *Please quote:* date of return, your ticket number
22. MAY 1987   and computer label number for each item.

THE YIN AND YANG OF ORGANIZATIONS

A Scintillating Guide to the Best in Current Management
Thinking

by Nancy Foy

GRANT
MCINTYRE

Dedicated to
JOHN WARREN STOKDYK
my favorite son, critic, historian, chef, and manager

First published in Great Britain in 1981 by
Grant McIntyre Ltd
39 Great Russell Street
London WC1B 3PH

First published in the U.S.A. by William Morrow and Company, Inc.

British Library Cataloguing in Publication Data
Foy, Nancy
  The yin and yang of organizations.
  1. Management
  I. Title
  658.4   HD31

  ISBN 0–86216–038–3

Printed and bound in Great Britain
at The Pitman Press, Bath

PREFACE

Man is a rational being. He organizes himself and his groups and his information into manageable entities. He then categorizes them, conceptualizes about them, analyzes them, and contrasts them. He creates language to do these things, and other languages to write sonatas and sonnets and computer programs and laws.

Man is also an irrational being, subject to feelings and emotions and responses he does not understand. He weeps at man-made sonatas and breaks man-made laws. He creates and responds to fashions and myths and taboos—to the extent that some feminist-conscious editor will no doubt try to rewrite this into "he/she" form.

Although the logical, analytical, numerate, linguistic faculties dwell in one half of the brain, and the intuitive, feeling, musical, symbolic faculties dwell in the other half, they are inextricably entwined in our everyday lives. Learning to live with both halves of ourselves, particularly in organizations, is the challenge that led me to gather up a number of disparate observations and try to put them into one coherent view.

Individuals, groups, and organizations can be categorized in many ways, most of them binary. We have male and female, extrovert and introvert, autocratic and participative, hierarchical and matrix, public and private, profitable and unprofitable, goods and services, hard and soft, cash cows and lame ducks. For each term (or "thesis") we immediately look for the opposite (or "antithesis"). It is usually easier to define something by describing its antithesis, just as it is easier to make friends by finding common enemies than by exploring the nuances of appreciation of common friends.

The thesis and antithesis, they say, can be resolved by synthesis. So it is with our human tendency to create opposites. The more I learn about organizations, the more I realize that people assume things to be opposite that need not be opposed.

Most of the really gifted managers I have known have had some instinctive knack of taking things that might seem to be 180° apart at separate poles (such as ownership of one's own ideas versus membership in a group or organization) and slowly bending the poles around, bit by bit, until they reached a more manageable 90° or less.

Sometimes I think these "organic managers" are people who can think in threes instead of twos, looking for some other idea or task to shift the polarized vectors. Sometimes they seem to do it by being so single-minded they simply ignore the dichotomies that bother other people. Whether the winning approach is unitary or trinary doesn't matter (another example of binary thinking!). What matters is that such people seem to be able to make their organizations work effectively.

"He" and "she" are different, but they are both parts of "mankind." The individual and the group and the organization are different, but they are all "living systems" with logical and emotional elements, conscious goals, and subconscious needs. Instead of discussing the individual *versus* the group *versus* the organization, we might gain more insight from looking for synthesis, for win/win games, for ways to make groups meet the needs of their members, or governments respond to the desires of their citizens. People need help in managing those above them, too. And from outside, consumers, environmentalists, and many others need tools to influence organizations. Those are the demands that will prevail in the rest of this century. As we can already see, the demands often take forms that don't seem rational, but the survival of groups, organizations, or even governments depends on meeting them, even so.

Every now and then each of us has a glimpse of our own subconscious reactions to something, but generally we prefer not to notice. (Psychiatry, in my view, amounts to helping people notice and resolve conflicts between conscious and subconscious demands.) Members of a work group either take for granted its unique behavior patterns or mores, or leave it. People inside a large organization are seldom aware how its culture and style and beliefs affect them, or how these differ from the cultures of other large bodies. Some of these things below the surface have to be made a little more explicit because people are more demanding now, and organizations will have to change a great deal in the next twenty years if they are to survive—and change, to be effective, must take into account the fears and feelings as well as the budgets and plans.

As we mature, we develop defenses against our own subconscious information because it doesn't always suit the self-image we have taken on from the mirrors of those around us. So it is with groups and organizations. There is a danger in making explicit some elements of their behavior which may be more comfortable left in the dark. I believe this danger is offset by the danger of leaving them below the surface, at the mercy of systems people who don't always understand living systems, or maverick manipulators who do. The individual who can recognize and respect both halves of his nature is better equipped to cope with change and with other individuals than one who must expend his energy defending the barrier between the two halves of his brain. And so it is with groups and organizations.

A great deal has been written about the logical, rational aspects of organizations. Because people inside them have become adept at the use of the often-esoteric terms in which such tomes are written, much of the information has become useful to them.

Somewhat less has been written about the soft, fuzzy, emotional, subconscious aspects of organizations. That which has reached the surface has tended to remain in the languages of psychologists or sociologists or behaviorists, languages that are more remote from everyday work. Thus, though the knowledge may exist, it is less accessible, and therefore less used.

The purpose of this book is to put other people's concepts, and my own, into the context of the real people who survive and thrive in organizations. If I concentrate on the softer, more social side, it is not to deny the importance of the harder, more logical side, but simply to reach toward a more balanced view of the two as equal portions of the human or corporate brain, as the yin and yang of organizations.

London, 1980   NANCY FOY

ACKNOWLEDGMENTS

I am indebted to Alan Cooper for encouragement and argument and for the title of this book, which so aptly combines the hard and soft, male and female, logical and emotional nature of living systems. I am equally indebted to James G. Miller for the concepts of living systems that have formed a structure for most of my learning in the past few years, to Warren Bennis for a human view of organizations combined with an impatience to accept their inhuman aspects, and to Reg Revans for the concepts by which people can control their own development.

I am particularly grateful to Philip Nind and the Foundation for Management Education in London, whose three-year research grant gave me the opportunity to think about these things, to Bob Tricker who was my mentor at the Oxford Centre for Management Studies, and to Alan Baddeley, Justin Dukes, Dan Samuel, and Michael Shanks who comprise the rest of an exhilarating steering committee for the research.

Friends and colleagues will recognize their contributions to my thinking. These include Jim Ball, Tor Blomquist, John Bridges, John Burns, Tony Carter, Richard Cochrane, Michael Dixon, Phil Dorn, Ron Edwards, David Ewing, Dick Foy, Peter Frankel, Bob Garratt, Saul Gellerman, Ron Halford, Charles Handy, Tom Lupton, Alistair Mant, Chris Martin, John Morris, Derek Sheane, Rosemary Stewart, Ann Stokdyk, Gerry Van Weelden, Roy Williams, and John Woolhouse. By concept, discussion, argument, and example they have helped me build a three-dimensional picture of how organizations work.

Although I am deeply indebted to many academic friends for other ideas and concepts, I shall plagiarize, paraphrase, and oversimplify them all as ruthlessly as possible to make this book useful to the people who must make organizations work. For those who are curious about the concepts in greater depth, I have included a long bibliography, but few notes or footnotes.

Most of all, I am grateful to the hundreds of managers and other people in organizations I have been able to talk to for the past several years, while I studied current and future management education and management development. It is their zest, their enthusiasm, their sense of challenge, and their problems of resolving so many demands that seem to conflict, that made this book imperative.

CONTENTS

Chapter 1.

THE DEMANDING FUTURE

Whatever else it is, the future for organizations will most assuredly be full of demands: demands from employees, demands from shareholders, demands from consumers, demands from regulators, demands from the media, demands from communities, demands from environmentalists, demands from trade unions, demands from middle management, demands from trade associations or employer federations, demands from government agencies, demands from volunteer groups, and so on.

From the chief executive officer's vantage point, it probably looks and feels like this:

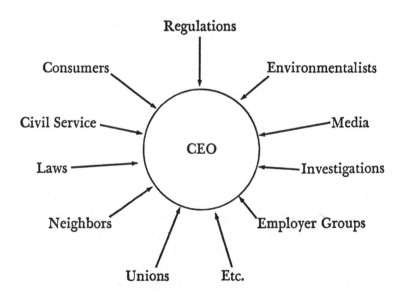

These and others keep pressing in, and in the process they're eroding the time he has available to run the organization. I've talked to a number who say: "I used to split my time about half and half between the inside and the outside, but in the last couple of years, it's closer to twenty/eighty" (or in some cases, "ten/ninety"). For the kinds of people who are chief executives, dealing with the outside used to be fun. That was where he personified the organization; that was where he had the rare chances to be himself with his peers, who understood some of the difficulties of being the place where the buck stops, the leader seldom able to control his own organization, powerless to change it. Outside was where he had a chance to pick up new perspectives to take back inside. Outside was where he refreshed himself.

It doesn't work that way any more, and it's going to get worse, not better. Now the outside is not refreshing but exhausting. Instead of picking up new perspectives, he feels himself going over the same ground for the fortieth time, to try to give outsiders some perspective from the company's viewpoint. He is at fault for things he and the company used to be proud of. He constantly feels guilty because so many of his people inside need a little more time, a little more attention, but the time and energy are being eaten up in all these outside contacts.

One trouble is that the chief executive, because these used to be refreshing contacts, tended to keep them to himself, or at best to share them with a tiny handful of top level colleagues. There were departments for public relations and external relations and industrial relations and government relations and so on to handle the more humdrum things, but he kept to himself the role of representing the company —and rightly so.

But the level of demands keeps on increasing. People are better educated. The world keeps getting more complex. Technology sometimes seems as if it's getting out of hand. Those better-educated people expect more and they have a tendency to create scapegoats when they are anxious or disappointed. Business is a favorite scapegoat in every industrialized country. And those more expectant, more articulate people are not content with words from someone in the middle of the organization; they want to hear from the horse's mouth. So the stress level on the chief executive goes up some more, to the point where something has to give.

This may be one reason so many organizations are gradually decentralizing. On the conscious side, the chief executive has to cut down the number of inside things with which he is personally involved, and that means slightly less control from the center, in a conscious decision. But there is also a de facto subconscious decentralization as he simply has to delegate the running of the business while his time is occupied with all these outside demands.

I believe these linked trends—toward greater intrusion from outside and greater decentralization inside organizations—will continue for the next decade or so. If they are, as I suspect, fueled by the higher expectations of the population, of consumers, of employees, of managers, of communities and so on, then the factors that raised those expectations are not going to change rapidly, no matter what the economy does. We have already seen "stagflation" and other phenomena that defy the descriptions of the mass psychology of another day and age.

The purpose of this book is to consider organizations, now and in the future, not to make predictions regarding economic trends. (Walter Heller once commented that economists learn very quickly to give a date or a number in their predictions but never both.) It might be useful, though, to remember that economics, like management, has just begun to emerge from a long period in which most people assumed a completely logical, numerate world. "If we could just get M3 right, the rest of the equation would fall into place." But individuals cannot be described in equations, and groups even less so. Many factors in "the economy" are actually dependent on the individual decisions of millions of people, and no matter how much we try to influence or control those decisions, people will go on being irrational, making their decisions on emotional bases, or finding ways around the systems we devise. (One reason the Russian system works, according to Hedrick Smith, is that a large proportion of it is actually a sort of "gray market" of entrepreneurial activity, called *Da Levo*—"on the left hand.")

Coming back to the level of the organization, we have the chief executive worrying about the economy as well as his own markets, products, employees, information systems, competition, and all that impinging outside world. A few seem able to respond and even go out into that world carrying the messages about what people can and cannot expect from business. Most are under stress, and some have ducked into a posture of waiting for things to return to normal.

That is not going to happen in the foreseeable future. One scenario from major international companies underscores the structural nature of the changes. (And because major international companies believe this is the picture of the future and will respond accordingly, it has some of the characteristics of a self-fulfilling prophecy; less major or less international companies will probably have to take account of it, too.) Here are a few of the points described by the late C. C. Pocock, who was chief executive of Shell Transport and Trading (and chief of Shell International's committee of chief executives):

* Slower real growth
* Persistent inflation
* Rising expectations
* Rising education
* Energy shortage
* Higher ethics and human rights demands
* Rising consumerism and environmentalism

Taken together, they make a daunting picture of a troubled environment in which "winning" is going to be even more difficult than before, and the best many companies will be able to do is "not lose." As we shall explore later, winning is fun; not-losing is not fun; and finding ways to put some of the fun back into organizations may be one of the greatest challenges for the future.

Several years ago Pocock headed an international committee to look at the needs for education and training of managers in the future, taking into account these gloomy factors (which seem to turn up in the scenarios of most futurologists these days). Their brief report offers some glimmers of optimism. The outside intrusions may in fact be bringing about more-human organizations, though there will be underreactions and overreactions as changes occur. But the more demanding employees will inevitably have to find their demands met in smaller work groups, with more autonomy. This means managers will manage in different (and ultimately more satisfying) ways, I think. The high cost of labor will lead to smaller, more manageable work forces, though there will certainly be an uproar every time a job or group or industry begins to dwindle visibly. There are terribly complex questions of job protection, job creation, and mismatch between the jobs available and the people who want to do them. But there are also intriguing new approaches on these fronts, and the rising concern about jobs may help fuel a trend to more satisfying work.

In twenty-five pages the Pocock report * paints a complex picture that merits closer attention. Although it was derived from the experiences of European companies, many if not most of the trends it highlights are also going to affect American firms in the future.

> * The social role of business is increasing. In the eighties it will be viewed more as the motor of the prosperity of society, as an agent for mobility and the development of individual talents, and as a stimulant of the "open society."

* Available from the European Foundation for Management Development, 20 Place Stephanie, B-1050 Brussels, Belgium.

* At the same time, traditional business decisions such as product lines, investments, and even hiring, firing, and deploying labor will be subject to more outside intervention. This means more social accountability and at the same time less direct control of employees and other resources.

* As power and authority roles change there will be trends in some countries toward unionization, consultation, participation, and "co-determination."

* Union power, which has been growing throughout Europe, shows a trend toward confrontation in the southern tier of countries, and toward consultation and cooperation in the northern countries.

* There will be a blending of shareholder and employee interests, with new ownership institutions emerging from such sources as government, unions, and pension funds.

* The gap between schools and business may narrow. However, it is clear today that young people with more education have new attitudes toward work that demand changes in work organization.

* Business is becoming more international. Managers in national companies will need more international know-how, and multinationals will give increased attention to national differences.

* Finance is becoming more crucial and more complex, with changes in ownership patterns, inflation, commodity prices, and purchasing power shifting into new hands.

* Control of inflation will bring a lower standard of living, high unemployment, and possibly a no-growth posture for industry. It will become virtually impossible to "export work" or to lay off workers or redeploy them freely, at least in Europe. Even with

widespread unemployment people will remain demanding as to the quality of job they will accept.

* Within large organizations we will have smaller, more self-sufficient work units whose managers may be more pro-active in dealing with elements outside the unit or the company. Projects, joint ventures, and other temporary links will increase.

* Higher technology, per se, may be less highly valued than "appropriate technology" that takes into account the social environment.

* Managers and other employees will expect more choice in the balance between work and nonwork, pay and performance, movement and stability.

* Individuals will take more responsibility for their own development. We will see less emphasis on teaching or training and more on un-learning, re-learning, and learning to learn.

* Successful senior managers will spend more time with people of different ages, backgrounds, and values at different levels, both inside and outside their companies.

* Managers will have to cope with many demands such as crisis management (or anti-crisis management), living with regulations, creating and dissolving temporary structures, harmonizing among conflicting interests and values, acting as links and spokesmen in the outside world, and building teams.

At the end of 1976 Norman MacRae wrote an important survey in *The Economist* giving a picture of a future in which the development of technology leaves man more free to choose what he wants to do. The groupings of motivated people who could operate in this environment would build fundamentally different organizations, less oppressive to their participants, less imperialistic in their relation to society as a whole. (People would be saying "Why?" instead of "Yes, sir.") Other experts looking into the future of organizations have carried this picture farther, depicting people involved in different roles in different groups at the same time. Such networks would be to some extent "public" where they made some contribution to society, and "private" in that they also met the choices and purposes of their individual members. Another aspect of the trend to more complex organizations will be an increased need to understand the subtle operation of power, to see how to influence decisions, and how to project visions of change in an environment that permits less dependence on coercion and hierarchy.

Demanding Employees

Changes in attitudes to work are increasing the demands on managers. Better-educated workers have higher expectations, and this challenges the traditional prerogatives of management. Already in Sweden a change in the laws regarding the "right to manage" has given the unions power to negotiate about virtually any management decision—and in any dispute the union is to be presumed right until proven otherwise in the labor court. Bob Tricker at Oxford calls this "the end of the deferential society."

When people are "at work" they are not necessarily working. We now see a shift in the center of gravity of today's power structures, and new demands are already visible in companies, unions, student organizations, environmental groups, government, and so on—the divine right of kings or managers no longer exists. But no one knows exactly how far out the power will move, or how fast. My own experiences with futurology (in high technology) suggest that we will probably overestimate the speed of change, and underestimate the breadth and depth of its effects on society.

In this context, people will expect, as a right, more opportunities to develop themselves and use their abilities; at the same time, stagnation and high unemployment will be creating fewer opportunities for them to learn through a variety of experience. In an organization that depends on moving people around to develop them, a shift in values toward job security can quickly clog up all the holes that were used to keep people moving and growing. This can result in staleness, boredom, inbred groups, or loss of cohesion. Educational leaves of absence may offer one way to loosen up again; these are likely to become standard practice in large firms, by law or by contract, at least in some countries.

Outside Demands

Broader connections inside and outside the organization will demand people who are expert communicators—but few employees below the top levels of organizations have had opportunities to develop the necessary skills. The demands for disclosure from all sides imply the ability to disclose and then translate information into terms that mean something to different audiences. The Freedom of Information Act has already forced the US Government to open up, and other forces such as consumerism and minority interests will expand this demanding environment. The person in the middle of an organization will have to become more aware of the outside, and to expand his time horizons.

Companies will have to satisfy outside demands that often conflict: to reduce unemployment, to raise living standards, to protect the environment, to contribute to developing countries, to help the handicapped, to make socially relevant products, and so on. Managers will have to understand economic, social, and political trends in much greater depth.

In a swirling constellation of government agencies, public interest groups, and individual citizens and consumers, the organizational survivor will need to listen, to translate, to bargain and negotiate among contesting interest groups. Industry's "license to operate" will increasingly come from the public outside, rather than its own economic performance. Industry will have to prove its legitimacy, its usefulness, its accountability to government and the public, without losing its efficiency and its profit-making ability. External relations will become part of the normal job of the normal manager, and the external relations portfolio will increasingly become a key development assignment for people destined for top management.

Demanding Managers

I've been describing some of the demands *on* managers; another important factor in the future of organizations will be new demands *by* managers. At every stage, from recruiting a raw manager-to-be through the mid-life crises to pre-retirement questions, there are new demands, and companies will have to listen and respond.

Many young people with ability today are not prepared to accept management jobs as they are presently constituted. Some are simply suffering from misconceptions about "big business" but many are turning away because their conceptions are all too correct. They don't want to be cogs in big machines. These are exactly the kinds of managers who will be needed most in the future, people with self-confidence and individuality who would rather use their social skills to engineer consent than to make all decisions themselves, people able to operate in a number of different environments, able to map different cultures. To recruit them we can't just create new advertising programs; we'll have to change the jobs they don't want into jobs that are attractive to them.

Middle managers are already showing signs of restiveness. Where will organizations find the commitment required for the top jobs of the future? How will companies demystify their boardrooms? How can we deodorize profit so it can be used once again as a yardstick of effort and excellence? Managers are asking themselves why anybody, including themselves, should obey an order. In Europe, part of the growth of white-collar unionism has been a trend toward unions for middle managers in large industries, a situation that will complicate the picture still further.

The world I describe in this book, of autonomous groups, of managers and employees able to take initiatives, of organizations that want to change themselves, of people involving themselves in networks and self-development, that world is *not* today recognizable to most managers in the middle. If industry is to survive, these must be the directions of its development, but the average manager today is far more constricted. What "management development" companies have is usually reserved for the elite, the fast-track boys. Very little has yet been done for the supervisors who are really the company's front line of contact with the shop-floor; instead, their jobs have more likely been impoverished and their autonomy has been eroded during the last decade. Every ten years or so the average middle manager (the "back-bone" of his organization) might be sent on a short course, but his chances to have a voice in his own development are low at best, and as a result many managers have stopped thinking of themselves as developable. Turning them back on may be one of the most important steps toward revitalizing organizations. They are already on the payrolls, simply an underutilized resource—but I am not very hopeful that the average company is likely to do a good job of developing the backbone manager in the foreseeable future.

One specific group of managers today merits particular attention. They might be called "the freezing forties." Middle managers, especially after they have passed the forty mark, are feeling squashed between the increasing concern for employees at the bottom and increasing distance from exciting changes at the top. They feel their careers have already peaked, and everything seems downhill thereafter. Even so, their power is immense, based on deep knowledge of how the organization really works; thus, while they may not be able to bring about change themselves, they nonetheless have tremendous capacity to block changes other people want, to paralyze an organization, consciously or unconsciously.

Finally, there are questions of what to do with older managers, those who are approaching retirement. With the legal right to go on working until they are seventy, many recognize that their work has been a vitalizing force; they look at colleagues who have retired to trivial lives and decide they will remain at their desks. How can their knowledge be better used? What kinds of patterns will we develop in the future to encourage "soft retirement" or part-time approaches that make room for others to move more freely without ignoring the needs of the preretirement managers? The "right" to go on working does not necessarily imply the right to go on having an interesting job, but it would be a waste of human as well as corporate resources to ignore this sector of the management population.

The Problems May Be Opportunities

Certainly, there are going to be legislative as well as social changes in the direction of more consultation, more participation, deeper negotiation about more aspects of working life than ever before. And the responses to these cannot be handled by the chief executive and his intimates any longer, simply because the changes are occurring across too broad a front. This means, ultimately, that the jobs of many other people, including managers, may be enriched (or complicated, depending on how you look at it) by greater contact with outside forces, as well as greater contact inside the organization.

Look at the middle manager's contacts today:

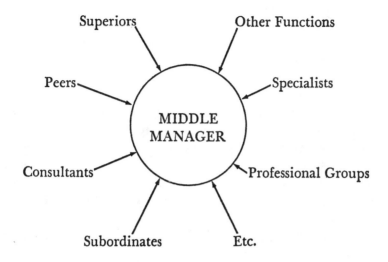

These, too, are increasing, and impinging on the time he has to do the job he believes is primary: running his own group or activity. Often he is less aware than the man at the top that his own role has actually shifted, that there is not likely to be a "return to normal," that he is, in fact, a "boundary manager" now and must delegate to others some of the internal things he used to enjoy doing himself.

"In the time we've spent talking about it, we could have done it!" That's a pragmatic manager's response to meetings, consultations, coordination committees, and so on. But in today's complicated organizations, it seems that most major problems come not from failures in "doing it" but in failures of coordination. "We thought *they* were supposed to be handling that." The boundary jobs are seldom licensed or authorized or made credible to the extent that they get done thoroughly, and more time is wasted in meetings and post-mortems to figure out whose fault it was, and devise infallible systems to prevent it (or a lot of other useful things) from happening again.

But management could actually be fun in the future if we handle things in a far-sighted way. Change is always uncomfortable, but look at the direction these forces are pointing: the chief executive is being forced to delegate more. Demanding employees are unwilling to work in soulless huge organizations. More women are entering the work force at various levels. The dependence on systems and techniques that characterized the sixties and early seventies is giving way to a stress on people skills of one sort or another. The modern shop floor is demanding new ways to have a voice in decisions that affect it. Work is getting more human, not less so. People expect a chance to learn as well as earn. Flexible working hours have already infiltrated large segments of business, making individuals responsible for their own timekeeping.

The manager in this environment will certainly need new skills. We've spent at least twenty years conditioning people to plan, measure, and control group activities; it will take a while to loosen up, to let individuals and groups make mistakes and fix them and learn from them, to shift the emphasis from control to coordination, from telling to listening, from measurement to sensing, from planning to nurturing. But many of today's managers already operate this way, and they are beginning to gain recognition for their nonstandard skills. Just as the scenarios for the future are already seeded in the fertile soil of today's corporation, so are the management approaches that will be most fruitful in dealing with that future.

So we have the problem of the impinging outside world, the demanding future. And we also have the opportunities to use this energy to speed up changes that are desirable for many other reasons. We have the problems of managing today and the opportunities to manage differently tomorrow. These are not opposites, or black and white outlooks, they are simply two organic parts of a whole. If the problem is an oil crisis the opportunities might be streamlined bicycles or selling solar heating systems or improved public transportation or smaller industrial concentrations closer to where people live.

Where the problem is managing in the demanding eighties and nineties, it is fairly clear that the opportunities are making organizations more human and encouraging people inside them, especially managers, to develop parts of themselves that have been submerged in the last several decades.

Chapter 2.

YIN AND YANG

Five thousand years ago in ancient China, Fu Hsi defined a philosophy that I find useful today to help explain so many paradoxes and dichotomies and balances in modern organizations. His "yin and yang" are still with us today in many forms. A modern writer, Nahum Stiskin, describes the polarity and integration of these opposites:

> Plants, man, and ideas all bloom in their season and wither in their season. Day changes into night, and night returns to day; the seasons run their course. Time, the enumeration of this change, stops for no man . . . Although at first view nature's poles present themselves as opposite and mutually antagonistic, on closer inspection we realize that they are complementary; one cannot exist without the other. Without the female there could be no male, and without the male there could be no female. The lungs both expand and contract continuously. If movement in either direction were to stop, life would cease. Were man to know no sadness, he would never know joy; without the experience of failure, he would know no success; without a knowledge of sickness, he could know no health. The universe and our knowledge of it are therefore constituted of the endless to-and-fro movement of life from any pole to its complementary opposite.

Philosophically, yin is female, yang is male. Yin is yielding, while yang represents primal power, energy, and strength. Yin is receptive, passive, while yang is dynamic, thrusting.

Stiskin defines yin as "centrifugal," moving toward the outside, while yang is "centripetal," pulled toward the center. Thus, yin is airy, yang is dense. Yin is vertical, yang is horizontal. In the electromagnetic spectrum, yin is the cold violet, while yang is the hot red. Yin is darkness, yang is light. Yin is water, yang is fire. Yin is air, yang is earth. Yin is night, yang is day. Yin is winter, yang is summer. Yin is vegetables, yang is meat. The relationship is not just male/female, but also prince to minister, father to son, teacher to student, or spiritual to animal. Yin is Martha, washing up while Mary (yang) prays. Stiskin says:

> The relationship of yin things to yang things is the relationship of magnetism. The north poles of two magnets repel each other; similarly, two south poles repel. But a north and south pole inexorably attract and hold to one another. Thus man is attracted to woman and electron to proton. Yin attracts yang, and yang attracts yin; yin repels yin, and yang repels yang. The force of mutual attraction (or repulsion) is proportional to the difference (or sameness) of the relative charges.

The Chinese believed that everything in the universe depends on these two processes being in balance, though it is a constantly moving, changing, dynamic balance. It is a useful picture for organizations; if the conceptual, intellectual yangs ran everything, things would gradually get out of balance, and analysis and learned papers would be its output. If the realistic, survival-oriented, pragmatic yins ran everything, it would also be unbalanced, and we would live in a world of ball-bearing factories. We need both, in moderate balance.

The feminist in me would like to argue with yin's dark, cold, passive, winter images, but it would be more useful to point out that the steretoypes have been with us for five thousand years and are deeply embedded in the stereotypes of most cultures.

Without odd numbers there could be no evens, and vice versa. These are poles, and in this context life, of individuals and groups and organizations, is a process of moving to and fro in harmony and balance between them. No one is completely yin or completely yang, but the existence of the poles may help us move about, as do latitude marks on a map, which derive their position from the chilly poles, even though most of us live within the temperate zones.

Right and Left Hemispheres

A few years ago William Domhoff asked many people to rate the ideas of left and right against other ideas. His respondents lined up this way:

left	right
bad	good
dark	light
profane	heavenly
female	male

The stereotypes persist. The intriguing thing is that in biology the sides of the brain are actually reversed; the left side of the body is controlled by the right side of the brain, and the right side of the body by the left side of the brain. These two halves of the brain, its "hemispheres," also correlate with the yin/yang and Domhoff polarities. For more than one hundred years doctors have been studying people who suffered brain injuries; as a result they have been able to "map" the brain and its functions to some extent (except for left-handed people, who are less consistent with these patterns). Each half of the brain can handle many functions, and both halves take part in most things we do. But as we grow up, our brains learn to specialize, just as individuals do; it is simply more efficient that way. So in most right-handed people, the left hemisphere is mainly concerned with analytical, logical thinking, with language, and with mathematical work. It works mainly in a straight line, processing information in sequence. It is the computer and it is also the yang element.

The other hemisphere (right in right-handed people) is

less adept at languages and linear activity. Instead, it is responsible for spatial relations, for arts, for recognizing faces and patterns, for holding an image of the body. Its information handling is diffuse, simultaneous, pulling together many facets at once. This is the emotional, feeling, yin element. Although, as noted above, the two halves are somewhat specialized, no one could survive without both of them. (The mapping has been carried out on people whose injuries involved loss of some but never all of a hemisphere.) In some cases, loss of capacity in one half, especially if it occurs early, can be compensated for by development in the other.

Robert Ornstein who has done an excellent study of the hemispheres, describes the interplay of the two in his own work:

> In the writing of this book, I have had vague idea after idea at different times: on the beach, in the mountains, in discussion, even while writing. These intuitions are sparse images—perhaps a connection which allows a new gestalt to form—but they are never fully clear, and never satisfactory by themselves. They are incomplete realizations, not a finished work. For me, it is only when the intellect has worked out these glimpses of form that the intuition becomes of any use to others. It is the very linearity of a book which enables the writer to refine his own intuitions, and clarify them, first to himself, and then if possible to the reader.

I believe that these two hemispheres, this yin and yang nature, also exists in groups and in organizations. I take my license for this belief from another conceptualizing writer, James G. Miller. His concept of *Living Systems* works at seven levels: the cell, the organ, the organism (which includes human beings), the group, the organization, the nation, and the super-national body. In his scheme of things, every living system includes nineteen subsystems, which process matter and energy, or information, or both. They are carefully named, as neutrally as possible, because specialists in so many different sciences that deal with living systems have evolved elaborate name systems of their own. Thus, the "decider" subsystem might be DNA in a cell, hormones in an individual, management in an organization, or government in a nation, but there is some opportunity to explore the function of deciding across those boundaries. The "boundary" subsystem, incidentally, might be the cell wall, a human's skin, a working group's territory with an imaginary line around it, the brick-and-mortar walls of a company, or the physical or legal borders of a nation.

Armed with these conceptual tools—the philosophy of yin and yang, the biological findings about hemispheres, and the concept of living systems that allows us to move up and down the scale of magnitude—we can begin to resolve some of the difficulties and questions that have evolved in several decades of organizational growth, dominated by "yang" approaches and high technology.

Many people in organizations these days suffer vague anxieties, impossible to pin down, but probably rooted in the essential unmanageability of large organizations that are leaning too heavily on the side of logic, orderliness, and analysis. We have to deal with the observable and perceptible world of reality and at the same time to cope with the imperceptible components, the things that we deem to be there but we can't see (such as human psychology or credibility or faith or organizational mythology). Half of the brain can cope with each kind of information, the other half can't. But the right hemisphere, the one that deals with the patterns, the emotions, the less logical portions, does not have a "license to operate." Thus, many of us, especially managers, are less confident in this realm, though the most gifted managers I've met demonstrate intuitive qualities at least as high as their logical abilities. The right hemisphere often has to express itself in the language of the left to cloak its intuitions in analytical words. This intuitive capacity in the right half correlates with the femaleness inherent in "yin." This does not at all denigrate women, especially in management; what organizations need, indeed, is to upgrade the capacity to deal with these invisibles, just as economists have had to learn to cope with the "invisibles" in foreign-trade calculations, or physicists have had to postulate invisible particles to explain phenomena that are otherwise inexplicable.

Licensing Intuition

By its very nature, intuition cannot be "taught." I believe it is trained *out* of people, especially men, from a very early age; like the capacity of the brain itself, a good deal of intuitive ability is present in most people; they should learn to trust it, to gain confidence in their intuitive insights. When two people are talking, for example, there may be a verbal message, and behind that, lurking in the muscle tone and tension of the voice, is a "meta-message" that tells what the speaker really means. It is the intuitive right hemisphere that can sense whether when you say "no" you mean "yes," or "maybe," or "no." Our cultural conditioning forces us to listen to the words, more and more, and our sensing of the meta-messages gets rusty with disuse. Babies are best at sensing meta-messages because they have no other cultural conditioning. Wives are better than husbands. Secretaries are better than bosses. And the top executives of most organizations are very poor indeed at sensing the meta-messages that come from those around them. Living lives that are overfull of rational information and dealing more with subordinates than superiors, they are trapped in a situation where the urgent left-hemisphere elements drive out the more important right-hemisphere signals.

Whether we're talking about an individual brain, a group's behavior, or the development of an organization, the interaction between the two halves is important. The notion of balance occurs in every realm. The ancient Chinese used to call it "eternal equipose." Engineers talk about a "beyond the center mechanism," such as a light switch, which tends to be either "off" or "on" but is very difficult to keep poised between the two. Recent studies of human biorhythms are based on the idea of active and passive periods, with a "critical" phase as the natural cycles (physical, emotional, and intellectual) move regularly from active to passive and back again. In Japan, if a bus driver has two of these cycles critical on the same day, he stays home; bus accident rates dropped as a result, and biorhythms of Tokyo bus drivers are now computerized.

This "on/off" critical element has a related concept in mathematics that might also be useful in thinking about the behavior of groups and organizations. The mathematicians talk about the development of "cusps" in disaster theory. Technically, this might be represented by the addition of one more battered Peugeot to the completely saturated Paris traffic system. Suddenly, everything clogs up completely. (I sat on a bus for two hours one afternoon, inching four blocks along the Champs Élysées.) With one less car, Paris traffic works smoothly. That single Peugeot is the "critical" stage, the cusp, the passage from on to off, the click of the switch. In organizations, I have seen intuitive managers who could sense the danger point, where a living system might click the wrong way—the addition of one more minor task to an overloaded group, or the imposition of one more procedures manual on an overcontrolled organization.

Different cultures handle the yin and yang elements of management in different ways. Because we have suffered years of imbalance, I think the current American interest in management in other cultures such as Japan could be useful, though there is no way one culture can be superimposed upon another blindly. But small manifestations of intuitive management might be helpful. Pascale gives an example:

> One of the most persistent afflictions in American organizations is the penchant to make formal announcements . . . The Japanese manager comes culturally equipped with a pair of concepts, *omote* (in front) and *ura* (behind the scenes). These ideas correspond to the Latin notions of de jure and de facto, with one impor-

tant distinction: the Japanese think of *ura* as constituting *real life*; *omote* is the *ceremonial function* for the benefit of others. The Japanese relegate the making of announcements to a secondary place that follows after all the action has taken place behind the scenes.

Organic approaches to management seem to fit the human ecology. You can make fertilizer in a laboratory, using a finite number of elements and reagents produced by the chemists and sold in carefully calibrated quantities. The process is delicate and expensive, but it works if you're careful, and there are usually only a few nasty by-products. Or you can toss your garbage and grass cuttings and autumn leaves in a heap in the back of the garden, throw on some dirt now and then, and let it take its own time. The compost heap produces better fertilizer, at no cost, without any ecological side effects—and it works every time.

Chapter 3.

MEN AND WOMEN

Women are not "equal"; they're different. This difference, which is really their greatest asset in organizations, is thrown away when they try to behave as equals and demand rights as equals. I realize this idiosyncratic view does not endear me to my feminist friends, but I'm as qualified as any other woman to have a view—and in the case of organizations, I will try to demonstrate that the difference may indeed make them *better* managers on occasion.

In a book-length debate about forecasting, Ritva Kaje exhorted her brethren to bring in the feminine or yin, "i.e., identify, acknowledge, accept, and deliberately develop the feminine qualities of all things." Her chart of yin and yang characteristics, reproduced on page 42, contains not only the stereotypes, but also the "ideal" mix halfway between maleness and femaleness, the place where balance is perfect —an impossible ideal but nonetheless worth aiming for in organizations that are overdominated by yang characteristics.

Intuitive Yin Qualities

I would contend that many women *are* more sensitive to underlying concerns, unstated objectives, and other kinds of meta-messages than the male managers who have become our stereotypes for success. In the systems era of the sixties a certain technical, numerate, decisive, macho image of management cast itself in concrete, without too much question in the Western world. But in the eighties and nineties, in which the individual demands of workers and managers alike will play a larger role, a "female" sensitivity will be important.

Female responses are often softer, too. Pascale, writing about Japanese and US managers, refers to the need to speak the stark truth, to "clear the air," as having a sexist component. He says:

> In our culture, simple, straightforward, simplistic confrontation—a kind of High Noon shoot-'em-out—is mixed with notions of what masculinity is. Unfortunately, shoot-'em-outs work best when the other guy dies. If you are obliged to work with that person on a continuing basis, such macho confrontations tend to complicate life immensely.
>
> In contrast, ambiguity, in reference to sensitivity and feelings, is alleged in the Western world to be female. But if we set aside the stereotypes and contemplate the consequences of these two modes of behavior on organizational life, we may discover that primitive notions of masculinity work no better in the office over the long term than they do in bed.

Biologically, I believe the female of the species is usually better equipped than her male counterpart to attend to detail. And she is generally willing to follow through, to mother a project, for example, for much longer, with less recognition. In the caves she tended the fire and kept the group together while the male went out looking for tigers to slay. In Viking days the women stayed in the flat, dull coastal areas of the northern countries, tending to the children and stoking the home-fires while the men went off across the North Sea in their longboats for a bit of winter

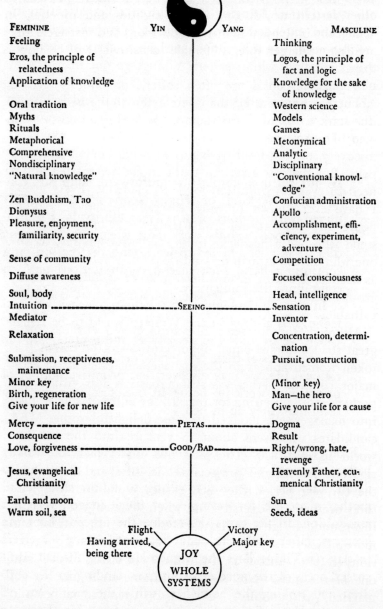

FEMININE	YIN	YANG	MASCULINE
Feeling			Thinking
Eros, the principle of relatedness			Logos, the principle of fact and logic
Application of knowledge			Knowledge for the sake of knowledge
Oral tradition			Western science
Myths			Models
Rituals			Games
Metaphorical			Metonymical
Comprehensive			Analytic
Nondisciplinary			Disciplinary
"Natural knowledge"			"Conventional knowledge"
Zen Buddhism, Tao			Confucian administration
Dionysus			Apollo
Pleasure, enjoyment, familiarity, security			Accomplishment, efficiency, experiment, adventure
Sense of community			Competition
Diffuse awareness			Focused consciousness
Soul, body			Head, intelligence
Intuition	SEEING		Sensation
Mediator			Inventor
Relaxation			Concentration, determination
Submission, receptiveness, maintenance			Pursuit, construction
Minor key			(Minor key)
Birth, regeneration			Man—the hero
Give your life for new life			Give your life for a cause
Mercy	PIETAS		Dogma
Consequence			Result
Love, forgiveness	GOOD/BAD		Right/wrong, hate, revenge
Jesus, evangelical Christianity			Heavenly Father, ecumenical Christianity
Earth and moon			Sun
Warm soil, sea			Seeds, ideas

Flight, Having arrived, being there

Victory
Major key

JOY
WHOLE
SYSTEMS

From *Futures Research: New Directions*, eds. Harold A. Linstone and W. H. Clive Simmonds, Addison-Wesley, 1977.

adventure before they came back for spring planting and other festivities. Bringing up children takes attention to detail and extended follow-through. These characteristics are also needed in the groups that have to carry on, keeping things running, while modern Vikings go out in search of new markets.

There are men who like tending to detail and following through on extended, thankless tasks. And there are women who like to venture out into uncharted seas for voyages of discovery, or join hunting bands to bring home some tiger pelts. But there *is* a certain truth in the stereotypes and a need in every organization for both elements. Every group I have ever known to work successfully had a "mother figure" of some sort (not always female)—the one who understood who had a headache today, and who was restive, the one who offered aspirin or sandwiches or emotional first aid as needed. Working groups need nurture as much as family groups, and if this is a female characteristic, it is no less valuable.

Although the women's liberation movement has made great strides toward equal opportunities—to the extent that token women appear in the management echelons of most major companies—there is still a barrier, less visible and perhaps more upsetting for that, to the entry of able women into management. I talked to some delightful young MBA candidates who were about to venture into the business world in mid-1979. The girls had undertaken the same rigorous courses and projects as the men, and throughout the two-year period they had earned equal standing with their brothers in adversity. But when it came to the recruiting round, the girls found they had fewer invitations and more silly letters giving them nonreasons for the noninvitations to follow through. "I think they're scared of us!" said one of the girls. "No, they just assume we'll quit to get married," said another. "As if all this time and money and work was just an elaborate modern way to grab a successful husband!" Although the MBA women were amused at some of the manifestations of traditional attitudes, there was a well-justified anger lurking underneath, especially for those who wanted careers outside the standard banking or personnel routes where women tend to be more welcome.

What Is Success?

A recent survey among more than five hundred female European management students revealed that almost 37 percent intended to go into finance or accounting, and more than 20 percent were aiming for personnel, followed by marketing (15 percent), and way down at the bottom of the list, production management (less than 1 percent). Of these women, 43 percent felt that it was a distinct disadvantage to be a woman, either because they were not seen as long-term employees, or because of more general kinds of prejudice among the male management population. Although they wanted to be judged on their own merits, they were quite realistic about the hurdles they would have to overcome to get into management. On the other hand, a large percentage went into management courses because they felt it would give them a better chance for interesting jobs. What they're saying, I think, is that we do have prejudice against women, particularly in the entry level jobs, but on the other hand, we don't have as much in management as you find in many other realms. About 10 percent of the sample were quite positive and optimistic that women are becoming more accepted in management, and companies are trying to right the imbalances of the past; however, as the students grew older the optimism grew less.

Another interesting survey by Nadelson and Eisenberg, two psychiatrists whose wives are professional women, highlights some of the obstacles for the woman who tries to combine family and career. Even the adjective "successful" is barbed; if it is used about a man it obviously refers to his working life, but a "successful" woman might as easily be the bandbox-tidy, entertain-husband's-boss little woman who takes her status from reflections of her spouse, rather than a woman who is successful in her career. They point out a funny thing, too, about the woman's view of her own success: although (or perhaps because) she has constant reminders that she is in a unique position in the organization, the successful professional woman is more likely to doubt her own worth than a man. She knows she is the exception to the rule, and that tends to reinforce the concept that women as a group are inherently inferior. The (incorrect) stereotypes that brainy is not beautiful and vice versa may increase her need to be loved for her beauty as well as her mind. Nadelson and Eisenberg say: "She is moving in realms where few women have moved before her, and she may doubt her legitimacy in situations in which men take their authority for granted." On the other hand, the husbands say (and I agree) that the quality of attention the children receive is better, and their opportunities to grow up with less stereotyped views of the roles of men and women may be a major advantage.

In my own experience and that of women I know, the few who carved out places for themselves in business did it in nonstandard ways. To go into a company's young-manager program and compete on equal terms and succeed on equal terms is unlikely (unless an Equal Opportunities impetus has given a reverse twist to the system). The young men who really reach the top, do so by means of mentors and short-cuts. Any analysis of men at the top reveals that their apprenticeship periods in lower and middle management were remarkably short. So it is with the women who make it inside organizations. They are usually (as are men in the high-flyer list) blessed with mentors—but this is a much more ticklish proposition when the spoken or unspoken accusations of favoritism have sexual undertones. Thus, for the mentor, it may feel a little more risky to promote the career of an able woman, while it would be perfectly normal to help develop a young man for higher responsibilities.

Sign Your Own Work

It is much easier, nicer, and more fun (in my view) to carve out your own niche without having to fight for niches that are defined by others and contended for by others. Let me give a few examples of women whom I consider to be successful, who found different ways to achieve success:

* Steve (for Stephanie) Shirley was a competent computer systems expert when she became pregnant. Unwilling to have her hours and maternity leave and so on determined by a company's policies, she started doing free-lance programming on her own terms. After the baby was born she discovered a number of other able women were at home with small children, wasting computer know-how that was in high demand. Starting her own company, she built it into a group of five hundred women that competes with the best in the world and often wins. Disgruntled male competitors sometimes mutter that she is able to underpay her people and work without having high overheads, because most of the employees either work in client locations or from their homes. But the real secret of success of the company, F International, is its better-than-average project management—and the fact that its self-employed "employees" are said to do an eight-hour task in their normal six-hour workdays.

* Marjorie Hurst, now in her late sixties, arrived at a meeting in her chauffeur-driven Rolls-Royce. At lunch she waved away the waiter ("I don't eat

lunch."), then the wine-waiter ("I don't drink."), then the fumes around her ("I don't smoke."). At that point she grinned across the table and said: "I don't have sex either. I just work." Her work involves running Britain's biggest bureau for temporary secretaries, a booming business that is constantly increasing because young women don't want to get caught up in organizational traps at the beginning of their working lives. Miss Hurst's organization gives them a trendy image with its advertising, and a sense of owning themselves with its vast assortment of short- and medium-term job opportunities. If you want to work half the year and play the other half, Marjorie Hurst has the machinery to let you do so.

* Communications careers have always been more open to women, and few barriers exist in journalism or advertising, where a skill with words is respected regardless of the sex of the person who possesses it. Judy Bloor, for example, was a fairly junior journalist on an accounting journal when her firm was thinking about a new computer journal. They searched for eminent men to take on the editor's post, and as the launch date approached, suitable candidates evaporated for several reasons, and Judy was thrust into the job, more or less as a place-holder until an experienced man could be found. She hired and trained a staff of people who were not originally notable for their experience in either journalism *or* computing. She did it so well that the journal soared into top position in Britain. She retired after five years. ("You can get trapped in a job like this," she said.) Today she is in charge of a new program for the same company to develop young graduates into top journalists and to develop all the existing journalists on the company's dozen or so magazines. It's

a "mothering" sort of job but it also involves planning, coordination, split-second decision-making, and delicate dealings with top executives.

* The academic world is another place where you are judged on the intrinsic merits of the work you do, rather than the manliness of the way in which you do it. Baroness Nancy Seear earned a life peerage for her work at the London School of Economics. Professor Enid Mumford was well known for her work combining systems and people insights long before she contended for a doctorate and a chair at the Manchester Business School. Rosemary Stewart at the Oxford Centre for Management Studies is known and respected around the world of industry for her work on the contacts and choices that really determine a manager's career. Angela Bowey at Strathclyde Business School has brought up five children while carving out her career in industrial relations.

My examples are British because I've been living in Britain for quite a few years, but the United States has many similar examples of women who have made reputations for themselves by starting their own companies or competing in fields where innate ability is the determining factor, and fewer sexual barriers exist—in short, they started from positions where they could sign their own work.

For four years my boss was Angeline Pantages, Connecticut-based international editor of the US journal *Datamation*. It was a marvelous experience, and she was the wisest, most driving, developing boss one could hope for. She also worked in an individual style that would be difficult for a large organization to assimilate—half-hour long-distance phone calls that would accidentally reveal not only how people's wives, kids, dogs, and gardens were doing, but also who was moving where to handle what project. Angie always asked the question beyond the question (*"Why* have you stopped beating your wife?"), often at 2 A.M. when her respondent was worn down. Her reputation as a night-bloomer with a sleepy look that didn't disappear until lunch-time didn't stop her from pouncing on odd facts and unintentional morning slips that revealed new nuances of the computer industry. In fifteen years of nonthreatening, noncompetitive work in the same job she became one of the most knowledgeable people in the world about this vital industry.

The opportunities are there, but they often require a nonstandard approach to be found and developed. And the management training we give both women and men tends to suppress nonstandard approaches. Therefore, the women who enter and try to rise through the normal channels do have an uphill battle. I have known more women who went into management from secretarial positions than I have seen go in through management-trainee assignments. The non-threatening secretary who has found an organization she likes has plenty of opportunity to learn how it ticks, what its fears and aspirations are, who are its heroes and villains, and how its various parts fit together. She still has a barrier to cross when she tries to leave secretarying and go into managing, but today an increasing number of companies are encouraging able secretaries to move into administration jobs that have wider horizons, and I believe the trend will continue.

For women, as for men, I believe the long-range key to success in an organization is the sense that you own yourself. Your career is ultimately in your own hands, not only in what you do in a particular job, but also how you handle the inevitable barriers to advancement. Women may need to change companies more often, because the number of places where women are not really welcome in management is still too high. On the other hand, the feminine ability to understand the undercurrents, to deal with the yin side of an organization, is a major asset, not just to the organization, but also to her own development.

The obvious way to increase the yin nature of an organization is to increase the role of women within it. Less obvious, but perhaps just as necessary, is to license the more feminine characteristics of its largely male population. To individuals and to groups, this may seem threatening, because the Western World has been entirely too successful in enforcing stereotypes of maleness and femaleness upon members of both sexes.

The current social trends, notably on the West Coast, toward more awareness, "relationships," and feeling may be spreading into business as well. Though it might be slightly absurd to work in an organization based on the Marin County precepts described in *The Serial*, there is certainly an increased emphasis on combining mind and body in some outdoors-flavored management or leadership courses, and the T-group phenomenon of the sixties and early seventies has given other forms of self-exploration and team-building greater acceptance and respectability.

Ritva Kaje suggests that groups can increase their yin nature if they go about it carefully and gradually, though it is difficult to let go of behavioral and spatial fixations such as conventional procedures, pecking orders, and structures that are petrified. Her recipe is to relax the group by exploring its models and systems, inquiring how the real system that underlies them is behaving, but leaving the old structures to wither away naturally rather than dismantling them formally all at once. "In applying any of these procedures," she warns, "one must beware of too much femininity —e.g., too much confusion—and strive for a balance which simultaneously brings forth masculine concepts such as structures and models."

For groups, as for individuals, there is a natural fear or resistance to "relaxing" in public, to revealing more of yourself or yourselves than you intended to, to others, or even to yourself. Before we can really increase the quality and quantity of feminine characteristics in an organization, its culture will have to give greater value to those characteristics, in men as well as in women.

Chapter 4.

FUN AND PROFIT

Gradually, during the last twenty years, we have been squeezing the fun out of organizations. The change has been imperceptible, a reorganization here, a new regulation there, more specialization in another place. The best way to track the change is to look across a generation to the children of today's mid-life managers. How many of them want to follow in the footsteps of their fathers?

Our offspring are more likely to aspire to be social workers or to return to the land and build simple, solar-heated houses; or they might fancy being paralegal aides in some public service group, organizing conferences, or working with disabled people. Too few of the best and brightest want to be managers in the traditional business mold.

A few years ago the *Harvard Business Review* ran an article about the changing attitudes of young people at American business schools. They were less likely to exhibit loyalty, to stay with a single employer no matter what. They were less interested in working long hours, or doing what the company thought was best. Remember, these were the young people who *were* interested in business careers, but already, by the early seventies, they were throwing up some basic questions. The reactions of most business leaders to this message was to demand that the business schools increase their brainwashing and put more emphasis on the good old virtues. Very few gave any thought to changing the jobs so they would attract able people, rather than trying to change the people so they would fit the existing jobs.

Where has the fun gone? I think it has oozed out from

between our fingers like quicksilver as we squeezed harder, looking for efficiency and growth, measuring success always by a bottom line, by this year's profit, even when it was achieved at the expense of next decade's vitality.

In government, in industry, in local communities, in school systems, in universities—every decision since the war has been in the direction of efficiency, and away from fun. Yet the two need not be opposites.

The Zest Factor

The importance of fun in organizations first came to my attention while I was sitting by a canal in an ancient European city after an international conference. We had had a marvelous time with a zany group of English, Dutch, and American colleagues. Too little sleep, late-night discussions that ranged from good ideas to good old war stories to two-part harmonies in several languages. "Why do the English war-stories always have such a slapstick element to them?" I asked a co-worker. "We know we won, so we don't have to rub it in," he replied. Suddenly, it became clear a fierce competitive sense was masked by that English understatement (the basis of most British humor). Stephen Potter with his "gamesmen" was simply codifying what every British schoolboy learns about one-upmanship before he's twelve.

Ernest Braun at Aston University refers to *homo ludens,* man the player, whose other facet is man the maker, *homo faber.* The more skilled we grow at cooperative, social endeavors, the more time we create for ourselves in which we might be playing. But we fill much of this time with ritual, to put further polish on those social skills that buy us the luxury of time. And those items we actually regard as our toys (from television to racing cars) tend to get wrapped around with high technology and ritual, as anyone who remembers skiing in the forties and fifties can testify. But at the same time, we feel guilty for having so much leisure and we tend to spend more of it in activities that don't polish up those social skills. Accustomed to valuing "labor-saving" approaches and "productivity," we may be caught short in our own achievements. Braun wants to see employment *and* enjoyment increased, or at least not diminished.

One aspect of *homo ludens* and his games may have various kinds of payoff in the future. In many ways he seems to be looking for patterns in many of his puzzles and games. There are economic patterns implicit in the business games. Or the biological patterns in biorhythms and other California-flavored phenomena. There are technical puzzles of varying degrees of elaboration, and now we have computers re-creating games we used to go out and play ourselves or sit in the rain with other people and watch. There's lots of renewed interest in arcane wisdoms contained in astrology or numerology. And within each specialism we have new games and models and puzzles, sometimes masquerading as "work."

What happens, though, if you take *homo ludens*, this gamesman, and put him in a situation where the best he can do is not-lose? If his zest no longer exists at work, he will have to find it somewhere else.

Winning is fun.
Not-losing is not fun.

Michael Maccoby's *Gamesmen* are American and they still exist in many companies, but their room to swing is inexorably shrinking. Potter's gamesmen are easier to find in pubs or clubs or boats or gardens than they are in offices.

I contend that the zest, the drive to win, the fun factor, is one of the most important elements in a good organization. It's an individual characteristic and a delicate one, but the organization that gives it room to thrive can thrive with it.

Ever since the war and the ensuing era of technology, we have been hemming in employees, especially managers, cutting down on their room to have fun. Even in sales, "winning" is much harder to define in large, interdependent organizations. Whole departments grow up to apportion out the sales bonus points among the different support groups that helped sell a big order to a big customer. The maverick who could beat out his opponent and bring home the order is more constrained today. Excesses of control and measurement and policies pointed toward fairness and equality have cut into an independent realm the gamesman could call his own. It's not so much fun these days.

The people who have suffered most are managers. Down on the shop-floor we can still have fun. If we think we're smarter than "them," we can steal things, or foul up their elegant systems, or simply indulge in a little industrial action. This gives plenty of room for individual fun and for group fun as well.

The manager, though, doesn't have these options. He's hemmed in by objective-setting and budgets, by demands from his bosses and his subordinates and his peers; but he gets very little fun in just meeting demands. Any bright ideas he has have to run a gauntlet of controls and committees, and to get them implemented he has to convince everyone else *they* had the bright idea.

Throughout society, there has been a general trend toward control, toward legalistic approaches to social problems, toward regulation, toward harmonization, toward standardization, toward bigness and blandness. We can't turn back the clock and start the postwar era all over again. But we *could* look for ways to keep what little zest remains in our organizations and we might even try, gradually, to increase it.

Images and Realities

One thing we could do is look at our organizations through the eyes of those children now growing up. All they see of Caterpillar or TRW or Upjohn is a tired father coming home. He probably doesn't talk much about his work, either because they wouldn't understand it, or because he needs an island of unwork in which to unwind. They don't pop into the office to see him because the office is buffered from the outside world by gates, guards, receptionists, secretaries, meetings, and agendas. They may know a few of his colleagues, but the small-company sense of community does not extend to the family of a big-company manager. It isn't surprising that many of these children get the idea that work in companies is tiring, bland, and boring.

In one meeting recently I took a survey among the ten past-forties lingering over their coffee cups. They had seventeen teen-age children among them, and only one of those was likely to go into management as we know it. That one was the offspring of the self-employed member who worked from home—so only one of the seventeen has been exposed from the cradle to the realities of work, the alternating drudgery and excitement, the fun of a new assignment, the distraction of a major report to finish, the meetings over the kitchen table to plot a new project.

The other turned-on members of the group had just as much fun and perhaps more diversity and excitement in their jobs (they were the exceptions that prove my anti-fun rule), but they weren't aware of the need to project these images beyond the boundaries of their big companies. And even if they were, the normal company is not an easy place to have families popping in and out. Going home every night and chanting: "I had a *great* day at the office today" isn't going to convince the average doubting teen-ager of anything except the innate absurdity of his parent.

Perhaps a bit of nepotism would help. Companies might, for example, make a greater effort to create interesting summer jobs for the able teen-age children of their employees. Most corporate summer jobs are dreary, pushing a mail cart or doing repetitive tasks no one else wants to do. They may be good for discipline and work habits, but the young people who survive them often come away disillusioned. Instead, why not create short-term, low-paid but interesting jobs, as apprentice to a busy and involved administrator or secretary. Or set a small team of capable young people to doing some fact-finding and feedback job that needs a fresh, outside view.

Even though the manager's room to swing has diminished, I believe that life in organizations is intrinsically interesting, because nowhere else can you find such a constantly changing kaleidoscope of people. They are at their best when they're focused on a shared task, and that is one reason we tend to talk in terms of profit, by which we are measuring some kind of shared achievement. But to people outside the organization, those profit figures, or any other esoteric measure we talk about that doesn't mention the people, seem to imply that the people are simply part of the machinery. Some of the fun, too, lies in the mistakes; too few organizations are willing to discuss their mistakes—and thus to laugh at them and learn from them.

Where the public image and the inside reality are out of step with each other, I don't think the answer is some kind of public relations campaign. It may entail family relations and some community relations to relax the public image. But if we want to entice our able offspring into organizational life in the next decade, we have to do *something* valid to make the organizations more livable, and then to let people see them in that light.

Win/Win Games

For one gamesman to win, we usually assume another has to lose. This is part of the management machismo, and the cost of win/lose games may be a factor contributing to the drop in zest. We can't afford to lose our losers (losing is most assuredly not-fun), and if someone loses face in an out-and-out, toe-to-toe battle, he will probably try to find a place somewhere else where he doesn't see "loser" in the eyes of everyone around him. So we cut down the opportunities to lose and the opportunities to learn, or win, as well.

One characteristic of Maccoby's gamesmen—and of many I have known in recent years—is the ability to have fun playing win/win games. Occasionally, you find a manager who looks for these purposefully, but he's still a rarity, and we aren't yet training him to do so, or instilling an appreciation of win/win gamesmanship in our corporate cultures.

Some games are by their nature "zero-sum games." If A gets the order, B loses it. If Germany has a positive balance of payments, someone else's must inevitably be negative. For every plus one party gets, another must inevitably have a minus.

Games that deal with money tend to be of this kind. But games that deal with information can be quite different. If I get a tidbit of information I know will be useful to you, and I pass it on to you, I still have the original information. You probably repay me in kind, either then or later, so I then have two useful bits of information, and so do you. We feel closer to each other as a result and will exchange information more easily the next time. We both won. (The corollary, or lose/lose game, is of course the one in which I withhold the useful information. When you get it from some other source, you probably realize I failed to pass it on, so you begin withholding, too.)

The prizes for win/win games are sometimes nebulous—good feelings or shared accomplishment—but they are often more important to people than money.

Conspiracy or Cock-up?

One of the things that keep people from playing these win/win games more often is their basic, unquestioned outlook on the world. If you think people are essentially lazy, out for what they can get, and worse than they used to be (which might be a paraphrase for McGregor's "Theory X" outlook), then you probably think you couldn't change much anyway, so you don't try. If you think people are essentially responsible, curious, willing to learn and grow for more reasons than money and you believe the world *can* be improved (the "Theory Y" outlook by which I've managed both my working life and my children), you may feel a bit battered now and then by the exceptions that prove the rule, but you are more likely to try to improve things.

These outlooks or attitudes or "theories" tend to be binary in the same manner that yin and yang are binary; few of us would be completely X or completely Y. We may move between the poles now and then; perfect balance is unlikely. But they are useful titles for understanding informal parts of living organizations.

The British have two terms for such sets of attitudes that rather bemuse me, because I see myself moving along the spectrum as I get older. One (the one I enjoyed in my younger years) they call "the *conspiracy theory* of history." Its adherents look for cabals, deep plans, and Svengalis pulling strings behind events in public or organizational life. As the seventies progressed and Watergate speeded up the opening up of many formerly closed organizations, the conspiracy theorists gained plenty of fuel with which to justify their beliefs.

The other theory (toward which I am rapidly moving as I spend more time around normal organizations) is called "the *cock-up theory* of history." A cock-up in Britain is analogous to a SNAFU in the US—an expression of Murphy's law (also known as "Sod's law" in Britain) that whatever can go wrong will. "For want of a nail the horse was lost . . ."

It is accidental events, including cock-ups, which influence the culture of an organization. A mistake today may seem unimportant, but measures taken to prevent it the next time may also prevent other good things from happening. People who can be identified as causing cock-ups are usually punished, overtly or unconsciously, and the ability to indulge in games, and thus to look for win/win games, is diminished once again.

/ 59

Monopoly Money

Money itself, in large organizations, seldom adds to people's fun or motivates them. Pay is rigidly, rigorously controlled, because you have to be fair to large numbers of people within the same organization. So you have various bands of job specifications, with matching bands of pay, and additional rewards for staying a long time. Getting a raise isn't fun, because it's seldom related to what you've accomplished, except in the negative sense, if you didn't get the raise you felt entitled to. The days when a boss could reward his subordinate by an immediate raise are past in most larger companies. You can sometimes be promoted as a reward, and that brings more money, but I think the real reward in promotion is the visible recognition that you've done a good job, that you've "won" in some fashion. After taxes, the monthly change in take-home pay is seldom enough to make a major difference to your life-style.

There is a great deal of evidence that money is simply one more counter in a big game, along with other symbols of recognition. I remember a three-year-old who pointed to his father's office building and said: "When I grow up I'm going to work in a corner office there and have my car right by the door." He had already figured out the counters in that company's status game. In one firm I remember the real pay for a promotion came when the interior decorator dropped in and you got to choose pictures for your wall from the next-level portfolio. In another company a female employee upset a number of colleagues by bringing into her small office a little rug and pleasant lamp. "If I'm going to spend one third of my life here, I'd like the surroundings to be pleasant," she said. The administrators muttered among themselves but let it go too long, and she won by default, somewhat diminishing the value of the carpeted offices that had been primary counters in the status game.

Status games really fall into the win/lose category in a way, because for one person to have status, another has to

60 /

have less status, though the effect is often diffuse, as in the balance-of-payments game. When the rewards are shared among a group of people and closely related to a task they have done, the win/win possibilities increase. And if the rewards come in the form of other tasks to be done, tasks the group (or individual) feels are important to others around it, then the entire organization gets a chance to win.

Often the zest factor is diminished, unconsciously, simply because the fun quotient in a decision is overlooked. If our processes of logical analysis and decision-making were augmented by a quick review of whose fun is increased and whose is diminished, we might be able to begin making decisions that put the fun back into management.

Chapter 5.

ENERGY AND ENTROPY

My favorite sculptor and I took a few weeks of creative holiday one year. I went out to the beach one afternoon, leaving her fiddling with a lump of clay. When I came back an hour or so later, she was putting the finishing touches on a little abstract torso. "That's magnificent, Mother," I said. "Don't touch it any more."

She smiled. "Ah, this was just the fun part. Now it will take six months of hard labor to make it in pink marble." As I headed back to the demanding typewriter, I remembered the old saying that creativity is 10 percent inspiration and 90 percent perspiration.

Creativity is really a cyclic thing, though. Before Mother could make that perfect model, she had dabbled for days with bits of clay and sat for weeks with a distant look, as images grew and clarified themselves in her mind. There's a kind of perspiration that precedes the inspiration that precedes the perspiration.

Creative Effort

Sir Maurice Kendall once wrote that his greatest creative contribution (which he considered to be a generalized solution for solitaire) came while he was mulching his wife's dahlias, after weeks of considering the mathematical conundrum. Christopher Strachey, the late computer theorist, once described his creative process as "immersing myself in everything to do with the problem, then going away for a couple of weeks in the country and not thinking about it at all."

At some moment, unbidden, the complete picture of the solution presented itself, rising out of unknown recesses of the brain to a place where he had access to it. Then, dropping everything, he would get it down on paper and keep working at the nuances of it, sometimes for weeks or months, until it was orderly, tidy, and completely sorted out.

As we are only beginning to learn today, the human brain has vastly more capacity than anyone ever imagined. Billions of billions of links between neurons exist, yet we have very narrow, tightly controlled ways of getting information out. Both hemispheres of the brain are involved in the creative process. I think those who achieve individual creativity are probably more adept than most of us at liberating some of the energy that all of us possess.

With its countless linkages, the brain can take in and store far more information than we know how to handle. Anyone who has suffered the indigestion feeling of "information overload" ("Don't tell me anything more—I can't cope!") will realize that survival depends as much on suppressing information as on getting it. So we grow skillful at developing symbols and words to denote huge realms of information, to keep it under control. Each of us has personal symbols and categories as well as those imposed by family, teachers, books, community, church, employer, psychiatrist, and special interests. To a large extent these symbols and categories are necessary, but they also limit our ability to process in new ways some of the information we already have. "Women are good at cooking" is a generalization that is valid for most people brought up in households where their mothers cooked most of their meals, but today it may limit a manager's outlook toward women as managers, for example, while the social climate demands an expanded view. The early model may overcontrol the brain's ability to bring more modern evidence to the surface.

Creativity has sometimes been called "bisociation," the ability to link together things that had not previously been linked. The concepts in Miller's *Living Systems,* for instance, help me move freely between cells, families, organizations, and individuals for examples that might shed light on a question. His creative and arduous work linking together seven different levels of living systems and enumerating their subsystems in language that is relatively free of the connotations of economists or biologists or psychologists or organization theorists gives the rest of us access to new symbols and analogies that can spark further creative processes. The "input/output" equations that are old hat to cell biologists, for example, are relatively new to economists.

I believe those who are able to be creative are not only exposed to a wide variety of inputs; they also seem to have a higher-than-average tolerance for not-yet-processed information, an ability to live with information indigestion without cutting down too sharply on the sense of yinlike disorder that comes with multiple inputs in multiple categories. At the same time, creativity needs some kind of yanglike outlet which the creator can wield with confidence, whether it be clay or paint or the written word or the flip-chart or the film or video camera or an ability to stand in front of a group and paint word-pictures. The outlet may depend on logical, learnable skills, but creativity itself also depends on intuitive confidence, following up hunches, sensing a congruence or connection that is not obvious to others.

Individual creativity is thus a delicate and complex process. Consider how much more delicate and complex it is, then, when it takes place in groups. People who may have the individual freedom of action to bisociate or create new symbols are often constrained by the narrower set of symbols shared by the group. Not only language but behavior patterns narrow, too, and the room to be "playful" or wander nonproductively is usually constrained. And yet we all know of examples of "synergy," the sum being greater than the parts, where a group was able to build up ideas that no single member could have linked. We need to explore further the constraints to groups—and the advantages they enjoy of wider knowledge and symbols, with potentially greater creativity.

Consciously and unconsciously, most organizations have set themselves up in a way that does not encourage creativity. This is sensible, because it would be chaotic to live in a constantly creative atmosphere, and without some kind of balance or control, an organization could not long survive that way. But somehow, as the technology explosion fueled an information explosion, I think we embedded too many of our controls in concrete, giving lip-service to creativity but trying to contain it in laboratories and constrain it to immediately identifiable products, markets, and services. We have been particularly reluctant to give room to the kind of creativity that might make these stultifying organizations work a little better. Again, a status quo we don't have to think about is more comfortable for most of us than a new approach that might (or might not) work better. Our group and organizational brains, too, need to impose controls for fear of flying apart in a chaos of information overload.

So we have agendas, procedures, standards, manuals, committees, reports, and goals and objectives, all the trappings of modern organizational life to convince ourselves that everything is under control. Some companies remind me of a terrified woman, working twenty hours a day to keep every speck of dust at bay and every knife and fork precisely in place, to keep at arm's length doubts about a dwindling self-image—and the more slavish her obsession with tidiness, the less warmth she gets from the few who must be around her, so the breakdown seems to loom inevitably.

I could picture also the opposite image, the orgy of creativity at the expense of order—and there are, or have been, companies such as this—with metaphoric unwashed dishes, mountains of newspapers, unpaid bills piling up, and no matter how creative the pursuit, when the disorder gets sufficiently out of hand the sense of failure descends (or the

TV gets repossessed), and things fly apart. Some modicum of organizational housekeeping is necessary in every company. The trouble is that systems are usually installed without automatic self-destruct mechanisms, and procedures left in place take on more importance than the events that originally caused them would warrant. So the average middling-to-large organization probably leans a little too far on the side of tidiness, if not obsessive orderliness, at the expense of its creative, intuitive abilities.

The Technology of Foolishness

In "The Technology of Foolishness" James March explores ways that organizations can make room for creativity without permanently disrupting systems and procedures and assumptions that give order to individuals and groups inside. Just as I am suggesting temporary systems and procedures, he suggests the temporary suspension of objectives, of "reasoned intelligence" to bring a playful element into situations in which people are in danger of thinking or behaving rigidly, in which they have learned too well the rational, logical approaches and the rules and procedures.

March defines playfulness as "the deliberate, temporary relaxation of rules in order to explore the possibilities of alternative rules." He goes on to suggest five new rules for injecting playfulness into too-rational processes:

1. Treat *goals as hypotheses*. Given a chance to experiment with alternative goals, "we stand some chance of discovering complicated and interesting combinations of good values that none of us previously imagined."

2. Treat *intuition as real*. Just because it is inexplicable does not mean intuition is worthless. It may be a way of reaching the other hemisphere, or of

avoiding highly programmed rationalizations that lurk in the logic of our beliefs.

3. Treat *hypocrisy as a transition*. He sees hypocrisy as an "inconsistency between expressed values and behavior." It is disapproved because inconsistency is uncomfortable, and because of "a sentiment against combining the pleasures of vice with the appearance of virtue." But the prohibition may inhibit change, and the hypocrite may be "a bad man experimenting with the possibility of becoming good," so the experiments merit encouragement.

4. Treat *memory as an enemy*. The ability to forget what we did yesterday may give us better chances to do better tomorrow.

5. Treat *experience as a theory*. Looking back, we can change our interpretations of experience (we do!). "Personal histories and national histories need to be rewritten rather continuously as a base for the retrospective learning of new self-conceptions."

March suggests that in management these might come into play by changing our view of objectives. Instead of viewing decisions as flowing inexorably from a pre-existing set of objectives, he suggests that decision-making might be viewed as a "process of gently upsetting preconceptions about what the organization is doing." Planning might be a constantly adapting way of interpreting past decisions, rather than a program for future decisions. Evaluation, which usually depends on predetermined criteria, should be turned around to take into account today's values, to discover new criteria. He thinks "social accountability" should include the use of imagination in forming social policy, not only to adapt to individual preferences but also to influence them by exposure to new experiences. And finally, he says, "The design of organizations should attend to the problems of maintaining both playfulness and reason as aspects of intelligent choice," particularly by giving people temporary relief from control, coordination, and communication.

None of us could afford to depend full time on intuition, to forget our experience, to suspend our goals. But exercises in organizational playfulness might help loosen up constrictions.

"Brainstorming," a game of free association among people who were accustomed to rational planning, once had this playful aspect. But in the nature of such phenomena, brainstorming itself began to gather rules until the title, at least, went out of fashion. It might be useful to resurrect it for exercises in playfulness, keeping the objectives as loose as possible and the debates about "what is brainstorming?" to a minimum. In this sense, it amounts to presenting a problem and getting people to suggest wild ideas. As these begin (always slowly) they are written quickly on a blackboard, and eventually the tempo speeds up—unless someone is allowed to analyze while the rest are synthesizing ideas. The slightest criticism can kill the process, and learning to suspend critical, analytical thought is part of the benefit of brainstorming. The manager who is too quick with reasons a subordinate's idea won't work doesn't get the benefit of further ideas, and the same is true among peers in a group that is brainstorming. So the only "rules" might be:

* Write down every notion that comes out.
* Don't sort or criticize while they're coming.

Later, the same group might happily disregard most of the notions, argue about a few, or even come up with different solutions entirely. The benefit should be in the exercise itself, the temporary playfulness, as much as in any "product" it comes up with. It may help loosen up a group to give it more room for creativity. Brainstorming gathered rather a hefty wodge of literature in the mid to late sixties; although there may be useful ideas in it, underlying most learned views was the assumption that the technique was to be used to solve problems. I'm suggesting it might also be used for the innate practice in suspending judgment and criticism and simply playing with ideas, for the long-term growth of a group, as well as its shared ownership of any useful ideas that emerge.

Freedom and Order *

In nature, energy and entropy coexist. "Entropy" in my personal definition is a kind of creative disorder, "heat," with atoms randomly bumping into each other, ultimately warming up the universe a little but depriving it of its sublime order. Energy, on the other hand, arises when the atoms are somewhat better focused, more orderly, tending toward the same direction. Linear accelerators and lasers demonstrate the effectiveness of order—awesomely. But the invention of such orderly implements was itself a less orderly process, occasioned by people bumping into other people and their ideas, building from one concept to the next, sometimes intuitively, sometimes rationally.

Inside the human cell, too, there is a randomness, with molecules accidentally bumping into each other. Enzymes bring a little order into the cell by attaching themselves to an element and staying clasped to it for long enough to bump into another element with which the first can make a useful link. I believe management of a creative group may work similarly, with the manager as an enzyme, gathering and developing people who can fit together to create something larger than any one of them could achieve.

In the cell, complete, linked chains of RNA or DNA replicate themselves with the help of random meetings and helpful enzymes and then move on to primary tasks. In the

* For much of this thinking I am indebted to Bob Tricker and his work on management information.

same way, if a creative group is to remain creative, it may experience gradually changing membership, or the occasional departure of a few members going on to do other things together.

The "enzyme," or manager, of such a group needs a unique combination of characteristics. At the creative, leading edge of an organization's activities, he needs to have credibility in its eyes for his mastery of its primary technology. At the same time, he has to have an intuitive awareness of the mix of elements currently and potentially useful for his group. These elements are people, and thus the mix includes emotional as well as intellectual blending. And he has to understand the complex, delicate process of perspiration/inspiration/perspiration by which a glimmer of an idea may be nursed to completion.

Most of all, the manager of a creative group must be the balance wheel between order and freedom, protecting his group on one hand from the incursions of tidiness from outside, and at the same time enforcing sufficient order inside that its energy can often be focused and made useful to the organization.

Model-Making

Let us return to the sculptor with her clay or an artist with paint and canvas or a man working with a linear programming model of the world's resources. They are making models of reality, interpreting it in ways that make sense to them and hopefully to others. But the models are not themselves the reality. Nor are models solutions.

The management literature is full of "models" that tend to be adopted slavishly. "John is a 9–1 manager," or "That is a Theory X organization." These models can be limiting or liberating, depending on how we use them. Some of us are more conceptual, others more pragmatic, and any one person shifts emphasis from day to day between these approaches. So one man's model may be another's "academic exercise."

Sometimes models can be helpful in sharing a picture of how things stand in an organization, or in getting people to talk about how they would like things to change. At one meeting, someone suggested that you could draw a model depicting the quality of managers; the first attempt looked like a barbell, with a cluster of gifted managers at one end and a cluster of poor managers at the other end, and a very narrow band of normalcy in between. Mant describes more of a Gaussian, bell-shaped curve, with the neglected majority, or "backbone," rising high in the middle. Such models might be useful in starting talk about how an organization ought to develop its managers and to give a sense of what shape the model might have if the development succeeded—but it doesn't tell how to achieve it.

In a related spate of model-scanning during my academic era, I found a number of seeming "opposites" (such as ownership and membership) that really belonged on two scales. Whereas ownership and membership seem to be particularly powerful forces at the working group level, another model describes the organization:

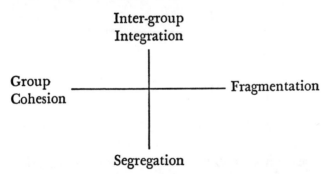

The literature of organization development (OD) is particularly lavish in its use of models. Peter Reason at Bath University uses a two-dimensional model to describe the role of the outsider:

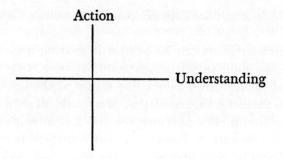

Action

Understanding

While managers tend to be more action-oriented, academics and consultants are often more concerned about understanding a phenomenon, but these need not be conflicting characteristics. The challenge is how to achieve high scores on both scales, and drawing the model may help people find new ways to do so. Often, on the other hand, the outsider, or conceptualizer, can have more influence than the insider, no matter how action-oriented he is, simply because change always involves risk, and the outsider can better afford the risk; his job is not on the line:

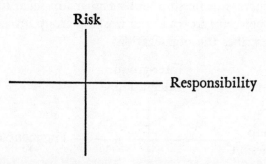

Risk

Responsibility

Similar models have been used to describe task or power orientations (and effective organizational change requires an awareness of both) or other organizational values and characteristics. These models are useful only to the extent that the people using them can see new relationships or challenges and then divert themselves from the oversimplified model to the complexities of real situations.

One set of "models" has irked me for years: the boxes with

which we draw our organizational charts. They imply hierarchy, even when the lines to higher and lower elements are missing. I try to use circles or hexagons instead, because they do not immediately demand hierarchical relationships, and the hexagon, placed next to another hexagon, often suggests the addition of a third element to focus the relationship of the first two. This is particularly helpful if you are trying to think of ways to make closer links with another element in an organization:

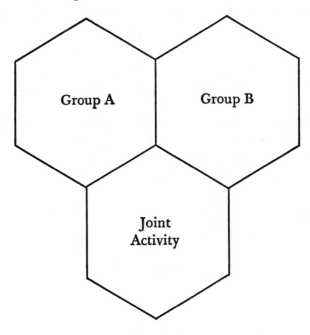

Some people think in pictures; others are happy with words or symbols. In the computer industry, early developments were hampered by the fact that half the systems were designed by people who used logic equations, and the other half by people who used logic diagrams, and the two had difficulty communicating with each other. They never tackled the communication problem directly; instead, each would carp at the quirks in the designs of the other (because the different "models" had different built-in assumptions). I believe the division still exists, even within companies where mergers have put people from both camps under a single roof. Those models were useful only within the groups that had shared a similar education, and they were counter-productive with those that had learned in a different way. Very few people ever took the opportunity to expand their horizons by learning the nuances of the other set of models.

Creativity occurs in the linked hemispheres of the brain of the creator, but to be useful it must find some outlet that is recognized in the hemispheres of other people.

Chapter 6.

LEADERS AND MANAGERS

Some people like to be told what to do; almost everybody likes to have someone out front, projecting an image of who we are and what we stand for. Ignoring all the elegant definitions of leadership and management that already exist in the literature, I should like to wrap my own around these characteristics. For purposes of this discussion, the person who is telling me what to do is my "manager"; the one who is projecting my corporate image (to me and to the world) is my "leader."

In this sense, it's a little like my grandmother's saying: "All ladies are women, but not all women are ladies." On the other hand, some of the finest leaders privately admit that they may not be great managers. "I'm just a cheerleader," said one who was on his way to the top. "I'm just a well-paid employee," said another, whose umpty-thousand employees might not agree on an egalitarian basis.

Instead, we might go back to yin and yang, or the hemispheres of the brain, for a useful distinction. "Management" in this sense encompasses the logical elements; it means getting a job done. In my lexicon, though, "leadership" also includes the emotional elements, some instinctive understanding of the personalities of groups and organizations, and how to strengthen and project them. The task changes very much as the size of the unit increases and may in fact demand quite different kinds of people at different sizes—but the leader is the one out front, the one who symbolizes the group or organization, no matter what its size. In part he is probably projecting his own personality, and if a good match exists between his own nature and that of his group or organization the larger element is likely to be better focused or strengthened. In part the leader also takes on its personality, emphasizing portions of himself that fit—and perhaps there are leaders who are themselves better focused or strengthened when a good match occurs.

Participation or Autocracy?

For some years debate has raged (in the delicate way debate rages in academic circles, and sometimes in management circles) about participative versus autocratic styles of leadership. At about the time I discovered that I was actually a "Theory Y mother" rather than simply too soft, I cast my lot with the participators and for years I, too, have preached the one true faith. Several recent experiences, though, indicate that the presence or absence of real leadership may be much more important than the style of any individual leader.

At one of Europe's leading management schools, for example, they have been taking data for some years relating the performance of syndicates or small class groups and the style of leadership that evolves in them. It didn't surprise me too much to find out that those groups which selected or elected truly participative leaders achieved most. But there was another curious item on the list. Those groups in which one member was a truly autocratic leader came within a hair of the first groups. In the first instance, the group seemed to agree on a shared style, either with or without help from a leader, and the leadership was mainly keeping track of who was going to do what as the members apportioned out the work among themselves. In the second instance, the members respected the greater knowledge or experience or forcefulness of one member, and by consent of the governed, he apportioned out the tasks and handled the coordinating, keeping things fairly orderly.

Then, as it turned out, there was rather a wide gap, and

two more group styles appeared at the bottom of the list: the fake participators and the un-credible autocrats. In the first instance, everyone agreed they were for motherhood (participation) and certainly against sin, but disorder reigned, and what they had was no leadership or coordination at all, rather than participative leadership. In the second instance, one member felt he had the God-given right to lead (and sometimes the group would actually elect him) but when it got down to cases (or flip-charts) he didn't really have the consent of the governed, and one way or another they would sabotage his authority, as his orders didn't make sense, or one member or another began to feel turned off.

The message I derived from this was that *the style of leadership is not as important as the personal credibility of the leader* (something my children might have pointed out if I had consulted them on the question).

Then I ran into a manager from a large American retail organization who fleshed out the picture a little more. "You're talking about tasks that were all roughly the same length, I'll bet," he said. "In short tasks with people who don't know each other well, the autocratic approach is often equally successful. But we've found that on longer tasks, the participative approach wins every time." Having determined this for themselves, the company then set out to make every manager aware of the difference. During in-house training sessions for managers, teachers act as leaders, and the usual competition between teams occurs. Half the leaders are very careful to get everyone involved, pass all the information around to everyone, and simply coordinate and keep the project on schedule for the hour or so of the exercise. In the other groups, the leaders give orders, apportion tasks with minimum consultation, and generally behave as a widely held stereotype of the modern, dynamic, goal-oriented, competitive, American manager. About halfway through, each leader receives an "urgent phone call" and the groups are left to themselves for about twenty minutes.

In the participative groups, the work goes on smoothly. In the autocratic groups, which might have been farther ahead in their tasks, it doesn't. The sabotage begins. Smoking is a case in point. In the participative groups, the leader starts by saying: "Incidentally, we better not smoke because the clean-air people are going to be using this room after us, and we'd better not leave it full of stale smoke for them." In the autocratic groups the leader simply says: "This will be a no-smoking area." As soon as the autocratic leader departs to "answer his phone call," out come the cigarettes; in the participative room there's no change. And so on—the exercise is full of little contrasts. The debriefing after the fact highlights for the managers how their own behavior differed under the two styles. The company reports that its attempt to change the overall corporate style has moved much more quickly since these sessions were added to the management training.

In a "leadership" course based on relatively autocratic assumptions, I had personal experience with the precept that participation works better on longer projects and a quick glimmer of insight that it can be disastrous on short ones with people who don't know one another. Perhaps to highlight the need for leadership, the organizers (the Leadership Trust in Britain) at the beginning of the outdoors-flavored course assign a team of six the task of moving water from one eleven-gallon barrel to another, across a twelve-foot space bisected by a burlap "wall" about eight feet high. The instructions are fairly complicated (the water cannot go around the ends of the wall, and tools and people go back to the start-point if they touch the ground in the prohibited area, and so on). Even more complicated is the array of pipes, scaffolding, and tools available to help do the job. Forty minutes are allowed from the moment a "leader" is appointed and given the instruction sheet.

Pandemonium! Reading it out in the classroom doesn't help much. We rush out into the field and look at all that daunting equipment. Several of the men immediately start seeing how pipes fit together, and whether they can arrange a scaffold. One girl cleverly gets herself onto the "wall" and then on a little island beyond it. Now what do we do with her? Pipes and a hose are waving this way and that; another woman scornfully says: "The boys are playing with Erector sets." She fills a pint-size plastic jug she found in the toolbox and throws it over the fence to her friend. Although two groups of three each were originally assigned to brainstorm and report back in five minutes, no one ever reported, and those groups have dissolved into three men building and three women throwing the pint-pot. At the end of forty minutes about two gallons have shifted, two more have been spilled, one man has bumped his elbow on a pipe, the men and women aren't talking to each other any more, and (as planned) the group feels as if it is a dismal failure. (The "solution," incidentally, was to poke the pipes *through* the burlap wall, but no one stopped to figure out the statutes and limitations.)

The lesson we've experienced is pointed out again: once the leader picked up the first pipe himself, it was a leaderless group and so it remained. The leaderly noises at the beginning did *not* help him (or us) find out whether everyone understood what the task really was, or how to apportion out the work. We used the entire time for brainstorming without ever homing in on which ideas were workable, and then planning how to do one of them. The task itself could have been finished in five or ten minutes if we'd used twenty minutes to think and plan. It was our first exercise and we blamed the leader—until each of us had a similar opportunity and discovered (in this unfamiliar, physical environment) that it's easier to philosophize about it than to manage it, much less lead the group. Even if we correctly apportioned the time for thinking and planning, it was difficult to get six people to listen to one another.

I'm not sure every member of the group saw it, but in the course of two days a natural leader emerged, and one appointed leader had the sense to subcontract the major part of a task (supervising the amateur construction of an aerial ropeway over a river). The woman to whom he delegated it knew no more about the task and did no more or better at the formal aspects of management, planning, and coordination that we were supposed to be learning about, but everyone liked to work for her. Her combination of common sense and team-building sensitivity were well suited to our needs at that time. I think the man who delegated the authority to her demonstrated another, and equally important, aspect of leadership: recognizing and using a "resource" of a more subtle, right-hemisphere sort than the pipes, wrenches, winches, and bos'n's chairs, which, as does hardware in other realms, so often deflect us from more important considerations.

Symbolic Leadership

My own style leading a treasure-hunt–type task turned out to be sociably haphazard, depending for success on happy accidents. In business, though, you can't count on happy accidents. There is also a difference in the requirements for managing a task or project and the qualities it takes to lead an organization during a long period. The particular quality demanded by the latter I would call "symbolic leadership," because so much depends on the leader's ability to project an image of the organization that suits and motivates its members. The image also has to appeal to the many other constituencies that impinge on modern organizations.

In my experience, the great leaders with the single-mindedness to carry out the symbolic leadership of large companies and the multi-faceted intellectual skills to keep track of all their activities are often unconscious autocrats, no matter what style they project for the organization itself. And if they are sufficiently colorful to make an impact on large numbers of employees, customers, shareholders, and others, their direct subordinates often seem willing to cover up for unconscious lapses in behavior that would be unthinkable in lesser mortals.

In one large company, for example, the chief executive was a man of personal ethics and repute who had created an ethical image throughout the corporation, long before today's emphasis on "social responsibility." Personal accountability was an important key to policing good behavior in the company; no manager would ever try to pass the blame to a subordinate for some mistake. But when his company was criticized by an outsider, the chief executive himself was likely to answer: "That was Bill Brown's fault," or "Charlie Jones should have taken care of that." Insiders suffered a touch of reverent exasperation, but it was real respect that kept any of them from ever pointing out the discrepancy between his own tendency to sell his troops down the river and the policy that no one else should ever do so.

Two men perhaps best known in the world for bringing participative styles to fruition (not only in their companies but also in their countries) are Johan Holte at Norsk Hydro in Norway and Pehr Gyllenhammar at Volvo in Sweden. Both seemed to me to be natural autocrats with their own subordinates, and often with managers generally, but both were also gifted at listening to people on the shop-floor, and setting an example for managers by so doing. In both companies the impetus for a shift to participation and consultation seemed to come from a "short-circuit" in which the chief executive made contact with people way out in factories and primary work groups, then came back to the center and directed the changes fairly autocratically. In both companies the workers felt able to influence decisions long before foremen and managers were similarly enriched. And in both cases I think the push/pull for participation speeded up the process considerably.

In changing their organizations, both Holte and Gyllenhammar used the media extensively, not just to talk about their companies but also to discuss the role of industry in society. Although such messages were generally interesting, they were also specifically informative to the thousands of people who worked for Norsk Hydro or Volvo. One manager mused: "I would go home and my wife would tell me what the company was going to be doing next; she'd seen the boss on television that afternoon." The ability to chat candidly and openly brought the personality of the leader into the living room in a way that no employee newsletter or communications campaign could achieve, and in the process a sense of shared mission built up very quickly. Gyllenhammar also wrote a book describing the changes in the company and the philosophy behind them, again using a candid and open style quite different from most business writing.

There seem to be contradictions here. People want to be led. But the participative style works best in the long run. But the leaders who have brought in participation on a grand scale seem pretty autocratic. I think the contradictions are resolved only by the personality and credibility of the leaders. It may take different kinds of sensors to hear what is going on within a single working group, or within a large corporation, but in either case the good leader *is* sensing the needs on the emotional side as well as the logical side. To do so on the grand scale you may need to be the kind of person who has some blind spots in the small-scale sensors. On either scale the leader seems to be able to create, amplify, and project a sense of mission and to personify the culture or personality of the organization.

Are Leaders Born or Made?

Many companies have done excellent work at learning to spot management potential and develop it. I don't think much has been done to identify and develop leadership potential. The leaders I have known were not just "entrepreneurial" (a characteristic that does *not* endear its owners to normal management-development programs or vice versa). They really seemed to have developed extra sensors, constantly taking the temperature or listening to the messages underneath the noise from many directions at once.

There may be an element of "self-fulfilling prophecy" in some development programs for high flyers. There is certainly evidence that people who make it to the tops of large organizations spend surprisingly little time in their middles. They may rise quickly to the tops of smaller organizations and then shift, or come in from other walks of life entirely, or else the organization is likely to have a fast track or an A list or some other mechanism for developing the cream of the candidates. It may be that knowing you are on the A list is sufficient impetus to begin developing those extra sensors. It may also be that spending too much time on intermediate rungs of the ladder dulls them for the larger task, perhaps by sharpening the sensors that deal with internal micro-politics. (Journalists know that if you want to find out about a company you ask either someone at the bottom who doesn't care about the politics, or the leader who doesn't care about them either. In between, people are too worried about what other people in the company would think, so answers are seldom clear or helpful.)

Some leaders, such as President Kennedy or Watson at IBM or Gyllenhammar at Volvo, were more or less trained for the job from the cradle. (This would be by the expectations of the parents, not of some organization; I have yet to see an organization train a great leader from the cradle.) More of today's leaders have emerged in adulthood, through more standard patterns.

A phenomenal 20 percent of the top three executives of Fortune 500 companies have had exposure to the Harvard Business School, which may be another form of self-fulfilling prophecy that encourages people to sharpen their own sensors as their expectations rise, no matter what happens to them in the actual educational exposure. On the other hand, with hundreds of people pouring through every year, has HBS been able to produce only three hundred or so leaders after all these years? Statistics depend on how you look at them, but in my view management education does not "create" leaders unless it gives people with potential a new vision of themselves.

Some of the tricks of leadership can be learned in an apprentice fashion, I believe, by exposure to fine leaders, providing the innate quality is already there. I doubt if more formal programs help except to intensify a sense of being elect.

There *are* tricks. Every good leader is part con man, part ham actor, part idealist, and sometimes even part philosopher. In writing about Japanese and American styles of management and communication, Pascale quotes one senior Sony executive:

> To be truthful, probably 60 percent of the decisions I make are my decisions. But I keep my intentions secret. In discussions with subordinates I ask questions, pursue facts and try to nudge them in my direction without disclosing my position. Sometimes I end up changing my position as the result of the dialogue. But whatever the outcome, they feel a part of the decision.

In the same set of interviews, Pascale notes an American who runs a ball-bearing plant in New Hampshire:

> It does not make so much difference if decisions are top down as it does how the top-down decision-maker goes about touching bases. If he begins with an open question, he can often guide his subordinates to a good solution.

In my own experience, the people who had this kind of sense and sensitivity, the ones I call "leaders," were *not* generally motivated by power. They may have been in earlier days, but by the time they reached the organizational stratospheres, they emanate a sense of responsibility and often a sense of zest, rather than an anxiety, about power. Perhaps, like money, power is most important when you don't have enough and becomes insignificant when you do.

Chapter 7.

WALLS AND WINDOWS

Every cell in the human body has a wall around it. The human organism is itself encased in a protective skin. The organization, too, has a protective wall around it, whether bricks and mortar or dollars and cents or its own patterns of behavior.

As do humans, organizations also have internal walls. For years I went along with the common assumption that these were unhealthy and should be broken down. Now I believe that the mergers and acquisitions of the sixties should have demonstrated to most of us that breaking down formal walls does not break down psychological walls. Indeed, they are probably just as necessary to the organization as the cell walls are to the human being.

In the past few years I have encountered surprisingly firm, impenetrable walls in a number of huge, successful companies:

* Unilever, the Dutch/British parent of Lever Brothers and others, is not broken down, as one might expect, into the Dutch and the British. I visited a friend who had been with their Wall's Ice Cream Company for more than thirty years; in a moment of candor he confessed: "I'm really a soap man." Later research confirmed that *soap* and *food* elements of the company consider themselves to be quite different.

* One secret of IBM's success is the wall between domestic and foreign operations. This dates back to

Thomas J. Watson's era; as his two sons and his company matured, Tom Junior took an interest in *domestic* operations, and his younger brother Dick became more concerned with *world trade* and IBM World Trade. The shape of the organization and the styles of the two elements followed suit in directions that suited both the personalities of the leaders and the needs of their markets.

* At Philips it was also the shape of the family that set the shape of the organization. The founder's son and son-in-law had different but complementary interests in *commercial* and *technical* aspects. To this day a Philips man will identify himself as first and foremost one or the other, long before nuances of his own specialism appear.

* Some Shell people, who might also be presumed to split into Dutch versus British, have mentioned instead a flavor of *exploration* versus *everyone else*. No matter how highly organized their operation, the explorers still have a tanned, virile, "sharp-end" image that sets them apart. The same may be true in the rest of the oil industry; one colleague who has been in the computer business for more than fifteen years still takes his image from oil exploration days.

These walls are impenetrable in that once a sense of membership in one part or the other descends upon a manager, he will happily wear that mantle for the rest of his life, just as a computer programmer will always feel most comfortable working in the first language in which he learned to write programs.

It would have been nice—and tidy—to claim that the strength of the walls increases as the size of the group grows smaller, or according to the length of time one spent inside a certain element. This doesn't seem to be true. I find a much closer correlation with symbolic leadership, especially in the early days of an organization. A strong personality is translated into a strong culture, which in turn creates a strong sense of membership, whatever the size of the element. A line manager who understands symbolic leadership can create this sense of membership in a smaller unit any time—sometimes at the expense of the sense of membership in the whole organization. One creative work group I remember clung together for years on the premise that the bad guys in some other department were out to take us over; the other department changed from time to time, as did the venue for after-work gatherings, as did the ownership of the firm, but never the knowledge of what we belonged to.

The sense of membership they confirm is lasting—but the walls are permeable, just as the cell walls permit nutrients to enter and wastes to leave, or the human skin and its orifices take in the feel, taste, smell, sight, and sound of the world around them. If we lose these senses, or our cell walls become less permeable; we suffer. Similarly, in organizations, there are ways to make sure the visible and invisible walls permit a steady flow of information, nutrients, senses, and people, as well as the primary inputs and outputs for which they are formally chartered. Our creative little work group was effective because the imagined threat of takeover drove us into constant in-house spying, or "G-2 work"; so we remained among the best-informed people in the company. If our reaction had been more fearful (or "reactionary") and the group been larger and less flexible, we might have pulled in our antennae and dug a trench around our area, thus cutting off our connections, making our formal output less effective, and ultimately bringing about the dreaded takeover.

The existence of a wall must be respected. If you bulldoze it down (as in mergers, takeovers, and reorganizations), it will continue to exist within the culture as an invisible demarcation, deluding newcomers and thwarting elaborate plans.

As anyone who has ever redone an old house learns, even unimportant-seeming walls sometimes have surprising load-bearing tasks.

It's much harder even to poke holes in walls, much less demolish them, than to build windows into them from the beginning. Often the light can be improved in a murky area simply by cleaning windows that already exist. The best way to keep organizational windows open is to use them like French doors, with people moving freely through them.

Informal networks can be very useful as windows in organizational walls. They permit information to flow freely as people move about, without endangering the sense of "home" within their own walls. Projects, task forces, and other "temporary systems" also have this merit. These are all discussed in separate chapters.

Two-way traffic speeds the process, with people moving freely out to learn about something, then coming home to think about it and discuss it, while outsiders feel welcome to drop in for similar reasons. This enhances both the information flow and the social process.

There are problems of course:

"How can we get any work done with all this meeting and consulting?"

"Whenever someone goes out, even for a couple of weeks, he's difficult for a while after he comes back."

For years I've heard the first complaint and wondered about it. I asked the question myself after spending some time in Sweden—but the results in the Swedish companies that do a great deal of consulting and discussing seem to demonstrate that the groups that talk among themselves the most also have the highest output. It's a group analogy of the old saying: "If you want something done, ask a busy man to do it." One university business school, convinced that its professors were spending too much time outside, began to tally their outside activities and found that the ones who were most involved outside were also the most productive inside.

The real productivity problems come when a group is trying to shift from a hard style of operation to a softer one (in yin/yang terms). Until people actually believe there is a new approach and have worked out ways of coping with their new ability to contribute, even tiny details will be thrashed out interminably. This is a natural phase of development (such as the small child full of trivial-sounding "Why?" questions), and one simply gets through it as gracefully and responsively as possible until the group has more confidence in its own abilities and consultation becomes more brisk. Several Swedish firms that have gone through this to the extent that the groups were clearly discussing *and* producing found the habit of longish meetings had built up. They speeded the process by rescheduling meetings for late in the workday, with a clear understanding that if they ran beyond the apportioned time it was people's own responsibility. Then there was no harm, and much benefit, if members stayed late over their coffee cups, simply chatting, at their own expense.

The re-entry problems from a longer assignment or task are somewhat more difficult. When someone has been out in an entirely different ambiance, thinking and learning about new topics, it is invariably disappointing to come back to the same old faces, attitudes, and activities, feeling oneself changed but unable to communicate the enthusiasm as well as the new ideas. This is particularly true of long management courses, which give managers a chance to view themselves and their organizations from a different vantage point and to compare their own ways with those of people from other organizations.

If individual refreshment or research is the reason for the assignment, then re-entry is simply something the individual will have to cope with, preferably having some chance to think and talk about it ahead of time. For extended assignments it often helps to have a mentor in the old group specifically chartered to keep the absent member up to date on happenings, help him make the move outward, and make sure his job (or a job or task that suits his new interests) is waiting when he gets back. In one large company this "career manager" watches over people on two- or three-year international assignments, and it is the career manager who gets the blame if the re-entrant is unhappy on his return. (A little accountability exercises the mind wonderfully.)

If someone is going outside on the premise that what he learns will help the group change and adapt to new circumstances, then it would be much more effective to send him along with a partner from the same group, so they can encourage each other on return and buffer each other from the deadening effects of the same old place. This is discussed in greater detail in the chapter on critical mass.

Sometimes walls hold people in against their will. In one California company in the sixties, the only way you could get a transfer to another department was to quit and then contend for the job from outside. I think empire-building is on the wane, and most companies are more relaxed about internal movement of a permanent sort, realizing how much cultural and political learning they are losing when able people have to depart to find new challenge. Nonetheless, pockets of resistance persist in almost every organization. A policy of posting all internal openings on all bulletin boards can make internal empires less fortresslike.

Chapter 8.

BOUNDARIES AND SPACES

A boundary can be as immovable as a brick wall, or as ephemeral as the line a child draws in the dust when he bellows: "I dare you to cross that!" I use the term "wall," though, to denote the demarcation line around a group or portion of an organization—a line that probably appears somewhere in the organization chart. A "boundary," on the other hand, may simply be the line an individual draws around his own sphere of activities, or the barrier one group of specialists creates, by speaking in esoteric terms, to keep outsiders at bay, across many organizational lines. (Computer people have been particularly guilty of this kind of boundary-building.)

As organizations have grown, systematized, become more complicated, and raised the levels of anxieties of many of their members, the number of invisible boundaries within and across them has grown. Today we need some tools for seeing boundaries and crossing them painlessly.

Many boundaries have existed for so long that we take them for granted, but they can baffle newcomers. Some are self-imposed and can become constricting. Some of the most fiercely defended and impenetrable boundaries in organization life are those between functions, where both the walls of the organization chart and the language boundaries of the specialists operate together to defeat the enemy (who usually lives right down the hall in an equally well-defended fortress). Hansen notes that managers in one large study could move from one company to another much more easily than they could shift from production to personnel, for instance. One of the people he talked to said:

> One's competence ends at the interface between functions. To venture across can be to reveal ignorance; to invite another across can be dangerous. For production to know too much about engineering could be risky for the head of engineering. Like the castles, knights, and bishops of a chess set who can only move in one set pattern, so do the managers. There is only one generalist, the president, and he like the queen dares to move as he wishes.

An individual's conscious or subconscious definition of his own boundaries may play an important part in his ultimate success—or lack of success. Every company has some example of an older manager who grows more and more defensive, locking up his know-how, or using it to block activities that might change his *modus vivendi*. In due course the organization finds ways to bypass him, and he defends a territory that is less important, whether it retains the same name and space or not.

I've met a number of lively managers who say: "Show me my boundaries and then leave me alone to operate within them." It's a healthy attitude and these tend to be effective people. Sometimes, though, they are less willing to grant to their own subordinates a similar freedom of action.

I was lunching with Frank Lucraft * one day, and another picture of boundaries emerged on the paper napkin as we sipped our coffee. Frank said: "No, that's limiting. If instead you could show me everyone else's boundaries then I'd have all the leftover space in which to operate." This is how he drew it:

* Hotel & Catering Industry Training Board, Altrincham, Cheshire.

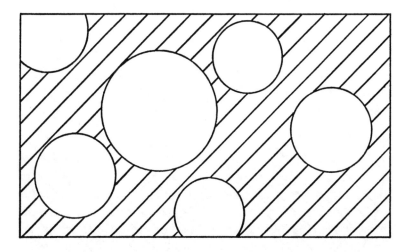

At another lunch, a year later, Mike Lidbetter * took up the problem of the subordinates, with a similar paper-napkin drawing. "The idea of delegation often gets confused," he said. "Most of us complain that we'd like our own jobs enlarged, but our bosses resist. In turn, we resist enlargement for our subordinates, because we've all seen examples of shop-floor enrichment causing the foremen or supervisors' jobs to become impoverished. But if you remember that your own job encompasses those of all your subordinates, you might draw it this way:

* Dunchurch Industrial Staff College, Dunchurch, Rugby.

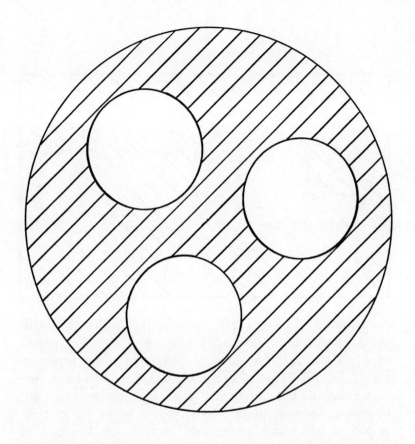

"Then, if their jobs are enriched or enlarged, you should have more time and energy to extend your own sphere. And these spheres, if I could draw them in three dimensions, would extend out, as much as up, so the organization or group as a whole would be able to achieve more":

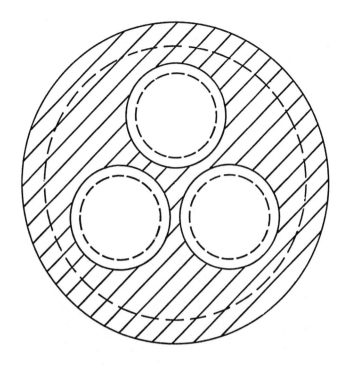

If other people's walls or boundaries are immediately adjacent to this element, it's easy to see that the manager who could not, in turn, enlarge his own interests would feel his own space diminished by the enrichment of the jobs within his sphere. But as long as there is room for expansion (which need not be territorial so long as it is rewarding to the individual manager and his group) this view of delegation might make a useful tool for group development.

That is a matter of enlarging boundaries. Crossing them brings a different set of challenges. The multifunctional manager must become multilingual. He has to be able to find out enough about the people in the group beyond the boundary in question to be able to discuss *their* problems and *their* situation in *their* terms. At the same time, in the other hemisphere of his brain, he has to map the symbols and feelings and fears that affect them, which may never surface in discussions.

Another colleague, Ron Halford,* contends that the manager shouldn't have any space of his own within his unit. He would draw it this way:

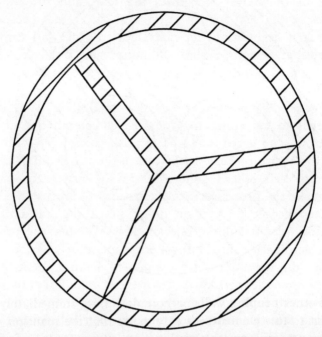

In this context, the job of the manager is two-fold. First, he should simply be moving around the boundaries, both inside and out, to make sure the others can work effectively, looking after the things that worry them, anticipating boundary problems and diverting them before they occur, and so on. This includes making sure that each is satisfied about his future, his pay, and all the other mechanics of organization life. Another task for the manager in this picture is being an amplifier for his people, translating and promoting their ideas to the world outside their boundary.

Several studies have pointed up the usefulness of focusing on a task, rather than roles; this distinction is particularly

* Organization Development Department, Pilkington Bros. Ltd., St. Helens, Lancs.

helpful for crossing boundaries. Anyone who has survived the niggling, what-if, t-crossing, and i-dotting negotiations between two bureaucratic volunteer groups trying to merge parts of themselves recognizes the fears and threats that power, status, and money inject into the formal process. I have seen negotiations for marriages and jobs fall through for similar reasons, where affiliations and linkages would have worked perfectly well and probably grown into lasting relationships.

If group A (or individual A, or organization A) believes it needs to get closer to group B (et cetera), one of the fastest ways to begin is to look for task or project C—though the task or project may be the reason the two groups needed to cross each other's boundaries in the first place—which can make the process even more natural. Then use the task to keep people focused on doing something, rather than ranking (or outranking) one another. Whether the project is an aerospace contract involving thousands of people, or simply the accountant who wants to learn a little more about how the personnel department handles entry-level training, it is important to reassure people from the beginning that their own areas of discretion and control and their own job security and status are inviolate.

The notion that people need reassurance should be regarded as a basic law of nature when it is scaled up to the level of the organization, especially when the project in question is some form of job enrichment, enlargement, or any other change that might bring flexibility to the organization by changing the nature of people's tasks. Any change that threatens a person's "territory" will be fought, and the denouement will be expensive at best.

There are perils in generalizing, because each boundary and each group and each organization is unique (which is another reason why business is so interesting). But acquaintance with a large number of organizations has helped me develop a few guidelines and *caveats* about crossing boundaries:

* *Pick the right size boundary.* One manager gave his people an inspirational pep talk about the need to expand their horizons, for the sake of the group, and go out and do missionary work among the unwashed, both inside the company and out. At the same time (thoroughly converted to the linkage cause himself), he encouraged them to do individual research on how other groups such as theirs operated. Very shortly his area was inundated with visitors and he began to exhibit the symptoms of information overload—glazing of the eyes, a lack of enthusiasm as new possibilities arose, and finally an attitude that said: "Don't tell me any more!" With a sense that things were getting out of hand, he clamped down on the outreach, limiting it to his two favorite elements—and the next time he tried, nobody responded. The moral is that too big a set of boundaries can be indigestible and self-defeating. At the same time, if the effort is too trivial, some individual may develop, but the group is unlikely to notice.

* *Informality is an essential ingredient,* especially in the early stages. Committees don't have as much chance to get to know each other as colleagues do. Despite management science, most innovative organizations know that the quality and quantity of innovation don't depend on the number of people but on their motivation—and the effectiveness of their informal links.

* *Visible early success helps.* If the first joint activity is viewed by the participants as a success—and especially if someone on high takes notice and commends them in some public way—they have a basis for further fruitful collaboration.

* *Make someone responsible for the boundary.* This carries a cost, because the person at the boundary has

to have visible (and often symbolic) support, as well as some discretion over his time, and the resources to build a network of links across the boundary. It helps to give recognition to people who have achieved new linkages, not only for the sake of those people, but also to develop the idea in the group or organization that such activities are valued. The recognition itself can often take the form of new boundaries to cross.

Like the problems of real organizations, the tools for crossing boundaries do not fit into tidy boxes. In my own language, they include finding out about the culture and problems of those across the boundary, finding people who are committed to bridging it, and finding projects in which both elements can develop a common interest. Money is seldom as much a limitation as are tradition and ignorance. Finally, finding new rewards for success in boundary-crossing can help build it into the value system.

Chapter 9.

OWNERSHIP AND MEMBERSHIP

The year my father died I was recently divorced, recently self-employed, and the children were away at school. With no patriarch/mentor, no family, no boss, no one else to whose drums I could march, for the first time in my life I was completely self-determined. I could work until 4 A.M. and sleep until mid-morning. I could eat popcorn in bed or leave the dishes till later. As long as I could pay the rent and school fees, I was free to travel wherever I could afford, to pursue any research that interested me, to decide my own balance between earning and learning.

The experience was exhilarating, but it also created anxieties. I began to fill up my diary with meetings and lunches, to fill up the empty house with friends and relations and cats, to take on larger roles in voluntary activities and networks, to spend more time with paternal clients in some kind of attempt to find an ersatz business home without endangering the new independence. I joined a "consultancy" that was really a dinner group of newly self-employed people; with all the effort it takes to achieve self-determination, we were still impelled by an anxious feeling that we "needed" partners. In short, I felt I had too much ownership of myself and my own activities and too little membership in something stable and recognized.

For most people in organizations, the balance leans slightly the other way. They would be grateful for a little self-determination, in working lives that are overdetermined by other people or by systems or by customs. On the other hand, they can take for granted the constant contact, the exchange of ideas, the support mechanisms, the typing pools, the copying machines, the coffee breaks, the "in" jokes, the internal politics, and the group achievements that convey a sense of membership.

I used to think that ownership and membership were opposite phenomena, that you either worked for yourself, or you belonged to the organization. Experiencing both of these and watching how different companies convey both ownership and membership to their employees has convinced me that the two are separate but not opposite characteristics. Indeed, I think most people need both ownership *and* membership. The young manager in a white-collar company who turns up in purple stripes is saying so. So is the real estate agent who joins Rotary, or the revolutionary student who spends his summer as a file clerk in local government.

It is to increase both the ownership of their own activities and the membership in small units that people in organizations build walls and boundaries. "We" can get on with things and control ourselves perfectly well in here while "they" are constantly trying to complicate our lives by making inconvenient decisions and changes out there. Sometimes an individual feels he has to defend himself from his own group in similar ways, perhaps making his job so mystical and complex and technical that no one else could possibly understand it, or creating a wall of forms or rules for protection. The underlying message is the same: we want to own ourselves.

The companies that are demonstrably good at developing managers have recognized this need for many years and used it to advantage. They take in able young people, often culling out the best for special attention, and then subject them to fairly intense acculturation in some rapid progression of apprentice posts, until they have enough membership in the organization to be let loose, either alone or in high-powered small groups, on special activities. The candidates for stardom are then personally accountable for their success or failure in a series of projects or new ventures—an experience to which most of them respond magnificently. In some firms it is possible to fail in some early venture and still climb higher; in others the fear of failure and knowledge of its consequences is a part of the motivation. In some companies the culture places a high value on cooperative abilities; in others competition is the keynote. But underlying all of them is the realization that the high flyers want personal recognition for their successes and a strong sense of owning the activities by which they are judged. Many of these companies lose good candidates through this process because they demonstrate less sense of membership than the firm would like as the sense of ownership grows.

One of the mechanisms that keeps ownership and membership in balance is movement. Insiders at IBM say: "IBM stands for 'I've Been Moved.'" There you stand or fall by the success of your project, but there's no sense building an empire because you won't be there to bask in it. Your reward for success is probably assignment to an elite task force; if you fail, you won't be fired, just forgotten, or retrained. Because *any* move is seen as a reward, people are more willing to move, though even in IBM younger people are today less mindlessly mobile.

Constant motion creates plenty of opportunities for development, but there are problems. Today most companies have to look for movement without relocation for many family men and to seek out the kinds of people who like moving, as well as recognizing the ages at which people prefer to stay put. And movement cuts into long-term responsibility and accountability. As phone users in the Boston and New York areas discovered in the late sixties, fast-moving Bell system managers were for years implicitly encouraged to stint on long-range investment in favor of short-term financial results, a policy that caught up with them when computer terminals arrived in large numbers to clog aging phone systems.

What is it that gives people a sense of ownership? Sometimes it is trivial things such as being able to come and go at hours of their own choosing. An important element is having some way of making one's own voice heard, whether it be a contribution to the creative process or a complaint about the working conditions, or consultation leading to a decision. Many companies have formal objective-setting or appraisal interviews; whether these help or hinder the sense of ownership of people in those companies probably depends on the informal beliefs about such mechanisms rather than the mechanisms themselves.

One example comes from IBM, which has a history since 1914 of trying to give individual employees ways of expressing themselves. In the early days, as with many firms, the leader claimed that his door was always open—which came to be known, in the nature of cultures, as the Open Door policy. In later years (as the Open Door was occasionally found to creak a little) new mechanisms came. Personnel specialists appeared to keep tabs on the contentment of the employees. A Speak-up column in the company paper was backed up with anonymous responses; anyone could ask anything and it would be answered. When the personnel people were considered not quite enough, Appraisal and Counseling (naturally known as "A&C") interviews were instigated throughout the burgeoning company. In more recent years, in at least one European country, a brush with the unions led to new grievance and appeals procedures, then the institution of Resident Directors to keep the company in closer touch with its communities, then Balanced Management courses throughout, to right the imbalance between scientific and human aspects of management. The last I heard, they were having Leap-Frog Lunches, at which managers entertained employees two levels down to make sure all the other systems were keeping the contentment levels high. It is easy to spoof these mechanisms, but they are genuine attempts to shorten the distance from the shop-floor to the boardroom, and the continuing attention to this aspect of management is certainly one of IBM's secrets of success. New mechanisms are needed every few years, but old ones seldom die; these are simply organizational facts of life anywhere.

Many of the same things that enhance the sense of ownership also provide a sense of membership, especially (as in the case above) where they underscore how "we" differ from other companies. Look at the language for the IBM mechanisms; each term arises in its turn and flows rapidly throughout the organization, until it becomes a normal part of everyone's vocabulary. You can go into a branch anywhere in the world and "Open Door" or "A&C" will mean the same thing—and that is very comforting for mobile people who are coping with strange customs in new parts of the world. Although the day of the paper collars or even white collars and gray flannel suits is long past, IBMers tend to dress in orderly, conservative ways. (The founder came from a hurly-burly world of traveling salesmen and wanted his employees to be as different as possible from their cigar-chomping, spats-and-loud-check-suited competitors, so they could enter the offices of bankers and company presidents as respectful and respectable servitors.) The reason for the sense of uniform disappeared years ago, but the indications of it remain in the culture, increasing the sense of membership in something special.

A good deal of the initial training companies give is also a way of creating a sense of membership. Those who take in most of their managers directly from college or university naturally have less trouble inculcating a distinct culture than those where people come and go more easily at various ages. Whether the high turnover is a result of too little sense of membership, or vice versa, the companies that acculturate their intake have certainly demonstrated that there is a correlation between the sense of membership and employee retention.

The membership sense may be born as well as made, though. I know of firms which consistently recruit what might be called "other-directed high-achievers," the kinds of people who strive to be president of the high school class or captain of the football team, without ever seriously questioning the values of the school or the team—or the company. When a company acquires a critical mass of such people and stirs them together in effective ways, the result is likely to be a concoction that is long on loyalty. If the intake is *too* consistently made up of earnest, programmable achievers willing to become full members of the team, it may be somewhat light on the leavening, creative, doubting elements who tend to develop their own values rather than accept those of the group. A few companies consciously encourage an easy-come, easy-go outlook for just this reason.

One ex-Shell friend refers to the company from which he escaped as a "fur-lined rut," saying he felt that the depth of training, shared language, and shared values made it difficult for members of the company to relate easily to outsiders. Shell is now making major strides to open up its boundaries, including the boundary to the outside—somewhat ahead of other multinationals, I believe.

Just as the doubter with his own values will resist too much membership, so a number of people are reluctant to accept too much ownership. Not everyone wants even limited self-determination, especially at first, as I learned for myself. It is uncomfortable; it creates anxieties; it demands that you take responsibility for your own actions in a way that few of us have been conditioned to enjoy. I spent years promoting the cause of shop-floor participation on the premise that everyone needed a slightly larger span of control of his or her own working life. As time went on it became clear that in every group there are members who see participation as a threat, not an opportunity. It also became clear that the consistency and credibility of a leader was more important to employees than whether he was participative or autocratic.

The overall demand for self-determination will grow, and I still believe that this is ultimately in the best interests of organizations as well as individuals. But I no longer believe we must impose a sense of ownership on everyone, any more than I believe that everyone deserves to be a member of something. Instead, we could be looking for ways to let people choose (albeit subconsciously) the degrees of freedom and belonging that suit each best, within the constraints of organizations.

Chapter 10.

SIN AND REDEMPTION

To have a sense of membership, you have to know there are people who are *not* members. If you live inside a wall, it's nice to know there are others out in the cold. A boundary isn't as interesting if there isn't someone on the other side, whether you dare him to come over or not. In other words, if we are to view ourselves as saints, there must be sinners.

The tendency to behave this way is universal; the definition of sin is not. In one company it's a sin to bypass the hierarchy; next door, in another company in the same industry, it's a sin *not* to bypass the hierarchy if something is bothering you. Here alcoholism or mental health problems are grounds for dismissal; over there they're problems requiring expert counsel.

The Catholic Church (which several friends have called "the first multinational") has a great deal to offer in management wisdom. They have small, highly autonomous units; a minimum number of levels of management; absolute authority on high for strategic matters, and plenty of power in the smallest parish for day-to-day operations. Both the yin and yang elements are incorporated into the faith as well as the practice. And they have an explicit and widely debated hierarchy of sins, with a matching hierarchy of punishments.

As well as keeping order, these "sins" probably also fulfill some human need to acquire and express guilt and then to expunge it. People whose primary allegiance is to other kinds of organizations probably have similar needs but very few business organizations have achieved the ancient wisdom of the church about human nature. So the ordinary organization has a less explicit (and therefore more anxiety-producing) sense of what is sin and what is not.

In most organizations, the only punishment for sin is to be banished, either completely by being fired or made surplus, or more passively by being exiled to some far-flung outpost where you never reappear in the inner circles again. In the olden days the personnel department was often a kind of Siberia for such banishments. "Once you've been erased from the A list," says one oil-company colleague, "you might as well find some other employer. There's no way to get back into the action."

This is wasteful. If we stop to consider how managers develop, or how people develop, for that matter, we find several intriguing factors. First, the ability to make mistakes early and at not too great an expense to one's career is built into the best development programs. Second, those companies which make people accountable for their successes—and their failures—seem to have more turned-on people.

The missing element in most companies is some mechanism for redemption from sin, a symbolic punishment-and-reinstatement system that puts to use the learning from the mistakes and the learning from the punishments.

One multinational, realizing the need for such a mechanism, invented one, simply by using an existing backwater in a new way. The formal title for the backwater was "The International Sales Center," a rather dreary building a few miles away from headquarters, which had once been envisaged as a place to sell things to foreigners, or give them snappy training courses. As foreign subsidiaries grew up and took over these tasks, the office languished. Finally, an executive who had been found guilty of a large organizational sin (a guilt shared by those beneath him, but personified by his leadership) was assigned to this backwater. For more than a year he did small tasks there, too loyal to question the company's wisdom, but sufficiently energetic to seek out other executives from time to time. Eventually, someone decided that he had suffered long enough and he was brought out, as if reborn, into a position that was clearly a development job even though its title was lowbrow. Soon after that, a foreign executive was guilty of getting in trouble with his country's government (making a speech for the wrong party), and a similar assignment was arranged rapidly; he returned in full honor when the government changed a year or so later.

By the time the third miscreant was assigned to the International Sales Center, people in the company were beginning to call it "the Penalty Box" and the hockey term stuck. Eventually, the pioneer began to include a description of his incarceration there in talks to young managers, inside the company and out, and the phenomenon of redemption became a full-fledged part of the company culture. His message was clear: "In this company, you can sin, atone, and go on to become number-two man."

After a period that is considered appropriate to the sin (which might be quite a long time if you want to go back to the original organization—long enough for some management changes to have occurred) someone somewhere deems the malefactor to have been rehabilitated, and he emerges from the Penalty Box, chastened and thoughtful, and goes to some new and often more challenging assignment. The insiders are notified by means of a demure notice on bulletin boards, and you have to be an insider to know that the transfer from an innocuous-sounding "X" to an equally innocuous-sounding "Y" denotes the re-entry of a manager from nothing to something important.

One reason redemption probably requires a near-formal mechanism, understood throughout the organization, is the persistence of images. So-and-so is held accountable for such-and-such, which has failed. Therefore, he becomes a non-person. It would not be too healthy to be seen giving him aid, comfort, and inside information. The trouble in most companies is that images have much longer lives than their causes, as we shall see when we discuss corporate cultures.

This kind of subconscious shibboleth can last forever, keeping the one-time sinner in a state of perpetual purgatory, even though he may have been reinstated in the eyes of his leaders. To overcome the image problem in a company that has no history of redemption, its leaders must go a long way beyond normal warmth to demonstrate that the punishment is over in every respect, and that the prodigal son has returned to the fold.

Where the Penalty Box idea exists, redeemed sinners usually come out to positions that are clearly recognized as development jobs. They seldom "turn off" while they are in the Penalty Boxes because they know from previous examples enshrined in the culture that they will come out "renewed," washed cleaner than clean. By remaining uncomplaining in their boxes they are proving their loyalty, expiating their sins, and presumably thinking about their experience and what they really want to do with their careers.

The payoff for such a mechanism can be high. Instead of losing good, turned-on people who are willing to take risks (and make mistakes), then having to replace them with others until the risk-taking element in the population has been tamed, the company can instead retain their knowledge of the culture, their enthusiasm, and their abilities. Indeed, it can also increase their drive to make achievements in the company's behalf.

Where should the Penalty Box be? I find that long management courses are sometimes used as Penalty Boxes, removing miscreants from sight for a suitable length of time without actually losing them—though the attrition for such people is usually high if the courses permit them to rub shoulders with people from other companies. This is another example of the punishment system and the reward system coming full circle, because long management courses are also viewed as rewards, often in the same companies.

There is unconscious banishment in many companies, simply out-of-sight/out-of-mind assignments for people who have made mistakes, or "don't quite fit." The individual in such a situation can sometimes turn his Siberia into a Penalty Box and re-emerge, but instigated by the individual this is an uphill battle. He can take the opportunity to learn new things, but he must also make superhuman efforts to remain in connection, to prove to the powers that be that he has learned, that he has become a worthwhile, contributing person. It isn't always worth the effort if the company doesn't recognize the merits of redemption, though the effort itself will help an individual develop and make him worth more to some other employer.

The personnel department should never be a Penalty Box in this day of demanding employee relations, though I still find companies that use it for banishment if not redemption. There are solitary bits of research that might be useful, or remote outposts where new energy might improve the local activity as well as the mind of the one to be punished. Remoteness is the key to the Penalty Box, as well as to Siberia; the difference between them is the ability to return.

Many well-known leaders—Jesus, Gandhi, Hitler, Churchill, Mao, Teddy Kennedy—have spent some time in the metaphoric desert, reflecting on and honing their views of the world. In years to come, there will be increasing demands from some mid-life managers to be rewarded for their loyalty with sabbatical assignments for just this purpose, to re-evaluate past experience and explore new directions. The "punishment" of a Penalty Box in this context need not be inherently unpleasant and can be potentially fruitful for some. Others may be lost—but they would be lost anyway once "punishment" was deemed to be the response appropriate to their actions. The few who are retained, who can learn from their mistakes, pay for them, and go on to be wiser leaders, can make the redemption mechanism worthwhile.

Redemption is important for more than just the leaders. The best development jobs are those in which managers have a chance to make mistakes, as most well-developed managers will testify. The other element in management development which is often overlooked is the importance of accountability, the chance to win or lose according to your own performance, in full daylight. But the organization that lacks a mechanism to punish people and then redeem them when they make mistakes will either drive them into not making mistakes—and therefore developing less than they could—or into not taking responsibility for their mistakes—and therefore developing less than they could. The companies that offer opportunities to sin and be redeemed, as do their counterparts in religion, are most likely to attract and develop ambitious, able people.

Chapter 11.

NETWORKS AND HIERARCHIES

We already have a large body of "information science" dealing with the technology of acquisition and retrieval of formal information and an even larger body of writing on "management information" telling us what it should be. The more we are swamped with information, the faster information science grows. Lurking underneath is a question that surfaces quite late, usually in the coffee breaks, at any meeting about management information: *credibility*. How do we get people to believe our formal pronouncements, printouts, bulletin board announcements, and annual reports? "You can lead a horse to water . . ." How can we, in turn, trust the inputs from our experts and systems?

The success of an organization may depend on how well it handles *informal* information—the grapevine, the jungle telegraph, and the rumor mill. Several studies have correlated long-term financial success with the richness of informal communications inside a company. I believe a similar richness outside the company's walls will also be important in the complicated decades to come.

When I was doing research about IBM, the portcullis went down, and most managers in New York, Paris, and London were aware that I was an intruder into the company's privacy. One day, hundreds of miles from Paris (in a small country where the formal guardians of the privacy had not thought to project their informal message), I sat in the office of the local manager and heard a play-by-play recap of an important meeting that had taken place in Paris the day before. His friend who had been there realized it would affect his operation and thoughtfully phoned him, telling him who was for and against the decision and how it might be easy to get around some of its sillier ramifications. I was more impressed by the speed and credibility of the informal network than by the content of the secret meeting. By the time the formal notification reached his far-away outpost, perhaps a week later, that manager would have mentioned it to the people who were affected, and their response would be brisk and effective.

That's one form of informal information. Someone in your network knows you're interested or affected and keeps you up to date. Another kind of informal information may be even more useful—the kind you didn't know you needed. A trend can sometimes be smelled the fourth or fifth time you hear a particular term within the same week. Someone mentions a problem over lunch and in your mind it becomes an opportunity for a new service or product. Your dentist and your commuting partner both overreact to a news item. You go on a course and find out that your personnel department, which seems like such a shambles, is actually coping better than most, as people from other companies trade horror stories after class.

This is the kind of information people trust, the kind that comes from people they know. When the informal information and the formal information are consistent with each other, people trust the formal information; when they are inconsistent, the informal information (or rumor machinery) wins every time.

You can't set up a system to increase the quality and quantity of informal information flowing through an organization. You *can* encourage the growth of informal networks, and strengthen those that already exist, inside and out. You can't plan a grapevine, or plant it, but you can fertilize one. It is no coincidence that companies that survive and thrive on their informal links almost never cut down on telephoning and travel, no matter how strict their budgets. At some subconscious level they realize that too-tight control ("Is this phone call really necessary?") would cost them more in the long run.

The Nature of Networks

An informal network can be as small as four or five people from different places who meet once for lunch and find it so rewarding that they decide to meet again every month. Or it might be hundreds of people in the same business who get the same newsletter and go to the same conference every year and run into one another in smaller clusters in between. Some professional societies claim to be networks, but the nature of such bodies is hierarchical, as we shall see, and the real networks are more likely to be local than national, under the formal umbrella of the society.

The purpose of a network is the flow of informal information. Once this idea is clear, the secrets of how networks operate are much more transparent. A company or public service body or professional society has other objectives and thus needs more formal mechanisms to maintain order and control, so it can meet those objectives. The people within those companies and other organizations, though, may be attracted more by the informal networks—the sense of being in the know—than they are held by the formal organization and goals.

Informal networks are particularly effective for the flow of informal information because they create windows in organizational walls, without damaging the sense of membership of people inside those walls. A working group without a link-man or butterfly is likely to suffer from information anemia, no matter how rich its supply of formal information through the hierarchy. If it doesn't hear through the grapevine that its output has been praised (or criticized) or that there is likely to be a problem about the arrival of some of its supplies or that a reorganization is likely next month, it can't do its job as well. The informal information contains indicators about the future, as well as informal facets of the present, or historical tidbits that help people understand the underlying culture of their organizations and others.

The informal network depends on the trust its members have in each other. In formal organizations, as in marriage, a primary demand is for loyalty. Thou shalt have no other gods (or wives, or chairmen) before me. But in networks, as in friendships, many links are possible, without endangering each other. I can belong to the Real Time Club, the local branch of the computer society, a luncheon group, an investment club, a great books group, a ski club, a teachers' association, an international personnel association, and still have fairly frequent reunions with members of two courses I attended and pals from several old firms. The number of other links actually enhances my value to the members of each network, because I can bring in more outside information and I become a link they can use, simply by dialing my phone number and asking a question, or stopping for a few minutes over coffee to mention something we're both interested in. Among the skiers is a good man impatient with his present job; among the personnel people is a director from a good company where the skier would fit better. The networks work because both of them trust my judgment somewhat, and even though they don't know each other yet, they both know my first name and face and phone number.

Journalists and generalists depend on networks. When you don't know what you're going to have to know about tomorrow, there's no way you can store up all the information about everything. So you operate by building a map of who knows about what. As you go on in this information-overloaded world, you may even have to refine it into a map of who-knows-who-knows. In essence you are mapping nodes into different networks; when the need arises, whether it be a research task about management development or a market opportunity in Nigeria, you begin with the primary nodes and work out into their networks, usually exchanging information or ideas in a *quid pro quo* as you go, using the telephone or visits as necessary. Once people know you better, you can operate mainly by phone and you become a resource to them in turn. But there is very little accounting in a real network, unless a member takes constantly without giving, or misuses information, damaging his sources in some way. Because it works informally, an entire network can dry up overnight if it's misused, as every journalist knows.

Specialists need informal networks, too. James Watson's book, *The Double Helix,* describes the informal flow of information that lay under the development of the Watson-Crick DNA model. "Creative" work often means putting together ideas from different realms; in their case some of the key information came from X-ray crystallography. Yet the specialist is more likely to be trapped within his own specialty in the formal hierarchy and less likely to find encouragement for links outside it. Not everyone is suited to the distraction of meetings, gatherings, lunches, and phone calls that goes with network membership, but even the most remote, abstract specialist may gain from access to a linkman who does belong to a variety of outside nets.

Most people belong to networks without having to call them by that name. The reason networks need to be described is to push their importance up into conscious realms; networks are delicate things and can be eroded or even killed by formal mechanisms and controls, whether those are imposed by formal organizations, or by the networks themselves.

No Goals

Though academics might prefer to call it an hypothesis, I think we have enough experience with informal networks for the flow of informal information to postulate a "law":*

*The effectiveness of a network
is inversely proportional to its formality.*

The more time members have to chat informally, the better they get to know one another, the more informal information they are injecting into the network and taking out of it. (One of the more interesting properties of information is that you don't lose it by giving it away.) As large companies know, every residential course is a de facto network, at least for a while, and courses that have regular reunions or alumni bulletins can often maintain their networks; most participants on management courses know that at least half the value comes not from the formal teaching and classroom discussions, but from the meals, coffee breaks, and sessions around the bar. If the "information" is no more elaborate than "I'm OK, you're OK" it is still valuable for building confidence.

The "membership" in a network, unless one abuses it, is almost completely in the hands of the individual. You are a member so long as a few of the other people at a gathering still recognize your face. If the membership turns over rapidly, as some do, you can always become a member again so long as you have the phone number of someone who knows where and when the next gathering is taking place. Your degree of membership depends on how often you meet other members and how much information you have for them.

The liveliness of a network, and thus its attraction to members, depends on the liveliness of the informal informa-

---

* At "morning after" meetings this is sometimes known as "Foy's law of the shared hangover." In that case it should be accompanied by "Burns' corollary" or the "principle of hydraulic balance." John Burns, my office-mate at Oxford and an experienced manager and management teacher, says that the teacher on a residential course can tell how good the session was the night before by the amount of water the managers drink the next morning.

tion. In the case of the lunching group of four or five, the few members are probably members of many networks. One network with hundreds of trainers works on the basis of frequent seminars and subgroups, but has no real barriers to entry.

A certain threshold of information flow is necessary to build a network, as RCA learned in the early days of color television. Until enough people could be attracted to buy color sets, there was little incentive for money to go into good color programs, and until there were good color programs, there was little incentive to buy a color television. In most business environments you can get over this threshold fairly rapidly by bringing together a couple of good speakers who don't necessarily agree about the topic and inviting as many people who know something about the topic as possible, then giving them plenty of time to argue with one another and the speakers. If they've had a good time and a new insight or two, they'll probably welcome the idea of regular gatherings. (The "new insights" are likely to be different for each participant, incidentally, and can't be programmed except by choice of participants.)

This "topic" gives the potential network its focus. *A network needs a focus, but not a goal.* As soon as you inject into a network a specific goal, beyond "keeping up to date about X" or "keeping in touch with each other," you are naturally driving away those members or potential members who have different or opposing goals, and their inputs may be among the most useful informal information for the members who *do* share the goal. To retain the integrity of the network for its primary purpose, let members use it to create their own subgroups for specific goals, but keep the network itself goal-free. I've seen several good networks lose valuable members when they decided to lobby for a particular piece of legislation; they might have kept the members and improved the laws simply by inviting various lawmakers along to normal gatherings, where individuals with varying views could do their own lobbying, thus giving the lawmakers more information and avoiding the trap of trying to create one uniform (and probably useless) formal view.

A network needs a spider at the center of the web, but not a chairman. Most networks of any size actually do have chairmen, and these are relatively harmless. Unless the chairman is also the spider, though, he is relatively less important. The spider's role is to build internal links, to keep the web touching enough different elements to retain its strength and balance, and to keep the information flowing across the network. The spider works not from a power role but more as a helpful assistant to the members. Dependable access is one of the spider's most endearing characteristics. Another must be some sense that the work itself is worthwhile, because few networks appreciate their spiders as much as they extol the virtues of their chairmen.

A network needs a note or a newsletter more than it needs a journal. A very small group may be able to convene itself by phone, but beyond five or six, a more formal mechanism is helpful (such as meeting on the first Thursday of every month). Beyond twenty or so it helps to have a reminder of meetings, activities, ideas, and new members. As is the network itself, the news medium is likely to be more effective if it is less formal. The seven-hundred-member Association of Teachers of Management (ATM) in Britain has an excellent journal, but its members are much more interested in the two-page typed news-sheet listing subgroup meetings, happenings in related networks, requests for information, and mentioning new members. Each monthly news-sheet also carries a few typed ads (paid for by members) for interesting jobs available among the industrial and academic members, thus enhancing the flow between the two incidentally.

A network needs a good list of members more than it needs a set of bylaws. I found out about one network because the head of a small company had a card on his bulletin board with the names, addresses, and phone numbers of thirty other presidents of local firms. "We do a lot more business among ourselves since we started this club," he said. "It cuts down on transportation costs, and I think I'm getting better deliveries because the guy you meet every month doesn't want to let you down." The purpose of the club is to talk about the problems of managing small firms in its region. Getting new business is simply one of those problems. I have found a tendency, though, for lists that could be useful to contain either too much information or too little. 'I seldom refer to the list from one network of two hundred members, giving all the details about each of their institutions; the book is too thick and lives in a bookcase in some other room. The short list with only first initials and company names is also useless, because I can't quite remember Gerald's last name or which of several companies he was with, and there are three possibilities with the initial "G." The optimum list for network purposes has his whole name and his whole phone number (including the extension number) for openers and probably his company or department and àn abbreviated mailing address if there's room.

A network needs groups rather than committees and they have gatherings rather than meetings. This is not to talk against committees and meetings; they have their place in the formal side and are probably necessary to achieve specific objectives. But they are hamstrung by chairmen and agendas, which constrain the flow of information to that which is formal and goal-related. A group meets because its members share some interest, and information flows because they have time to talk informally to one another. As many groups (including some good boards of directors) have discovered, both needs can be met if sufficient time is left in the agenda for coffee, meals, rest, and relaxation. As with organizations, the effectiveness of the group, if it is working toward a specific goal, may depend as much on this informal process as it does on the formal action. A formal organization or group can also *be* a network, so long as it respects the separate needs of the network.

A network needs an annual bash rather than a convention.

Most annual bashes are called conventions or conferences or reunions or something else, but from the network viewpoint, the need is for a symbolic gathering of at least a critical mass of the faithful, at least overnight—an opportunity for the shared hangover or the feast or the annual poker game or any other mutually accepted symbol of their occasional but ongoing togetherness. No doubt there is formal input or output to justify such an occurrence, but it has been my experience that in any network of more than twenty it is probably the informal contacts that are most valuable and keep the network alive. If a network doesn't have some such ceremonial gathering at least once a year, its links are likely to grow pretty rusty, and livelier subgroups or supergroups that do convene regularly will supplant it. (That's not necessarily a bad thing; I doubt if the manufacturers of quill pens have annual trade shows any more.)

A network needs a phone number rather than a building. As Parkinson has pointed out, the edifice complex can be deadly. In smaller networks the tasks of the spider can even rotate, so long as all members know where the central node for information can be reached.

The moral of the story is simple. Hierarchies need order; *networks need minimum bureaucracy.* The two need not be conflicting requirements, so long as the flatness and voluntary nature of the network are respected, and time is allocated to be unallocated. Most effective networks in business have to operate within psychological and organizational constraints. We are somehow unable to tell ourselves the whole truth—that we're going to a gathering because it's fun and probably useful as well. Our accountants demand a modicum of proof that it is a business meeting, and our consciences demand that we work very hard to compensate for enjoying a set of new or favorite faces. But if we lean over too far on the side of orderliness and control and achievement, we may cut out the zest that brings the members of a network we most wanted to see.

Managing Upwards

The same idea of voluntariness is useful for those willing
to undertake the challenging game of managing those above
them. Those approaches that depend on power and coercion
—industrial action, for example, or work-to-rule, or any other
strength-in-numbers action—may be effective but they are
based on the idea of conflict. And the basic notion underlying my philosophy about organizations is to minimize conflict, to cut down on polarization, to look for games where
everybody wins. So the crux of managing upwards skillfully
is to help those at higher echelons make the decisions you
believe are best for the organization. This requires all the
skills for management downwards plus an extra modicum
of sensitivity and tact (which would be nice if they were
exercised in downwards management too, of course).

* You need to listen delicately, hanging your chosen
  decisions on threads of existing ideas, attitudes, and
  issues.

* You need to give the "managed" up there plenty of
  information, so they can feel they are making up
  their own minds.

* That information will need to be specially congruent
  between the formal and informal systems. (Secretaries
  can still move a great deal of informal information
  into executive realms.)

* It takes considerable patience to plant an idea, watch
  it germinate and grow, to fertilize it as necessary, and
  see it through to fruitful harvest. And if you've done
  it successfully from below, you are unlikely to get
  any credit for the achievement, though it be considerable.

Because of the last item, it is sometimes helpful to build
your own support system, so long as it remains quite in-

formal. At the first whiff of a "committee-for" something from down in the ranks, many managers are likely to react like Pavlov's dogs with an attitude against. On the other hand, if you have the ear of a manager who has decided to implement your idea, and he asks for help, you may be able to plant the idea of a committee-for as an excellent example of his participative management style. Make sure the committee or support group is powerless and contains beloved members of the group, and you're most likely to succeed in the long run. From then on, whatever the outcome you want, achieving it is simply a matter of good networking, once it has obtained management sponsorship.

Managing upwards is probably more difficult when the subject is not a new idea or project but fixing some ongoing thing, or dealing with some prickly personnel situation. If a key man is about to be fired or transferred or head-hunted, all you can do is invoke the informal information networks to alert those on high to impending implications and how people below feel about it. Your main insurance against such events is somehow to maintain clear and open channels to several people on higher rungs of the hierarchy, to give them good news ("People down here are really pleased about your new policy to . . .") as often as possible, and to develop some trust and interest on their part in informal aspects of the organization.

Chapter 12.

SPIDERS AND BUTTERFLIES

Spiders and butterflies, * though vital to the ecology of an organization, normally receive too little recognition for their services. This may happen in part because their tasks, though they involve the flow of formal and informal information, are not usually carried out in a way that enhances personal power. In fact, success in either role requires the kind of personality that does *not* hoard information as a basis for power.

The spider, in my terminology, is the weaver near the center of a web or network of relationships, who tends the net and keeps it alive and useful to its members. The butterfly, on the other hand, flies around the boundaries of organizations and networks, gathering information from many flowers and pollinating others in passing. The tasks are remarkably similar, though the spider tends to be more rooted in a single place. They might be characterized as:

The spider is the one with the card file.

The butterfly works from a little black book.

Consider the role of Marguerite Greatorex, a spider who tends a network of a few hundred professionals. She sits in a tiny office in a lowbrow local college, working mainly by

* While butterflies seem to have only positive emotional connotations, spiders are the subject of phobias in a few people, and their images are not generally as benign as I intend here. I retain the term because web-building is the crux of the task, but my organizational spiders are not black widows, simply hardworking, helpful, near-invisible garden spiders, the kind whose webs can best be seen in morning dew and sunshine.

phone. A member phones in with a question about the international meeting. "It's at four Thursday," Marguerite says, reminding him that Dr. A, who is also interested in the proposed trip to China, is going to be there. As she goes back to the last editing of her newsletter, the phone rings again. Another member wonders whether she knows someone in his early thirties who might be able to take on an interesting job. "He really ought to be able to become my successor." Marguerite scratches her head, mentions a couple of names, and asks if she can pass the opportunity around informally among a few others. Then she rings another member to ask her to attend a meeting of another organization with slightly overlapping interests. "Give me a call and let me know whether we ought to be taking a closer interest," Marguerite finishes cheerfully.

Underpaid and overworked, she gets some recognition from the members, more so in recent years as the network has grown and membership fees have been able to support a part-time assistant for her on the clerical side, and computerization of her invoicing task. Now she is able to attend a few more of the subgroup meetings and often contributes information about other members who know about questions that arise, though she is otherwise mainly silent, helpful about arrangements, able to find an overhead projector or flip-chart holder on a moment's notice. She gives the impression of being a loyal servant—but the network would be dead within six months if it had to run on volunteer energy.

In my experience, spiders are often female. This may have something to do with images of manliness and management, which would actually be counterproductive in supporting networks. (In truth, many effective organizations with strong leaders, inside companies, are actually enhanced by the gossamer threads woven by a skilled secretary, supporting the leader.) One spider is a mother who returned to the work force in her thirties. Another at twenty-four graduated gradually from a secretary's job, where she became de facto spider before her skills were recognized. Yet another is a homosexual man, supporting an elite network of powerful colleagues who compete with each other. Although he is a full member of the network, his self-effacing handling of the arrangements and muted professional participation earn him the kind of taken-for-granted status that many dutiful wives would recognize.

However (in keeping with the move to liberate women), it is time the self-effacing spider had a little more recognition. First of all, the increase in the supply and demand for information will mean more of us need more networks in the eighties, and thus we will need more spiders to build the nets and keep them mended for us. Furthermore, to attract good people who are able to thrive without personal power and its manifestations, we might as well get some practice in bestowing a little recognition where it can do us the most good. Finally, by taking a closer look at how spiders work, we may be able to translate some of their skills into those needed for organizational survival in the eighties.

The skills of the spider revolve around the ability to keep a great many facts and people sorted out. The spider knows who needs to know about what and which two members shouldn't be seated next to each other and who deals best by letter and who by phone (invariably the spider is in his or her element on the phone) and where we could get access to a good library and who owes $24 for the last two meetings. It's the kind of job in which the information helps you make friends, not enemies, because the spider can only build his or her net by getting members in every direction to keep an eye on their own portions of it and let her know when some corner needs a bit of mending. Anyone who has ever tried to manage a volunteer organization would recognize the magnitude of the task—it takes twelve phone calls to get two people to drive the Cub Scouts to the picnic Saturday, and even at that, you need a standby driver just in case. But when the spider is a paid employee of the network rather than a fellow volunteer, it is that much harder to get some kinds of assistance that are necessary.

The spider also has a skill for quietly enhancing a sense of membership, for remembering the small events that can be built into traditions, for calling something the "second annual . . ." instead of just putting out a notice about a special meeting. He (I shall use the term in the interest of sexual equality) has to build a reputation for being helpful, for knowing the answers, without turning people off by demanding too much in return, or knowing-it-all. Yet this helpfulness can too easily be taken for servility; I remember one network of which the chairman expected the spider to bring breakfast on a tray during the three-day annual conference. (Chairmen come and go; spiders, hopefully, go on forever.)

Against this backdrop, the butterfly is perhaps more fortunate in having wings. The information processing is similar, and similarly dependent on people voluntarily contributing information because the person is seen as helpful, but the butterfly operates on the move. Lunch tables and committee rooms and other people's offices and the social areas around big conferences are his (or her) natural habitat. While the stationary spider builds a web for the members, the butterfly moves about in other people's networks, building his or her own personal, loose network, usually of "who-knows-who-knows." He might be a salesman or a journalist, a head-hunter or an account executive; he makes his living from his reputation for being able to find out if he doesn't already know something or someone. Sometimes he is directly buying or selling information (as in journalism), but usually his motivation is really curiosity; he may be the perennial student or gossip or dilettante who has found some way to live around organizations that gives an outlet for his natural style. You are more likely to ask him where you can find a good management-development man than to hire him for the position. His expertise is in the knowing rather than the doing. He is likely to be creative (if he's able to operate beyond the confines of a single specialty) but he's best paired with somebody else for follow-through.

The trouble is that butterflies, trying to please by contributing their helpful bits of information, don't fit into the normal power scheme any more than spiders do. And being butterflies, they are likely to fly away if they feel underappreciated, simply because they know so many other people in so many other places who might be more respectful of their contributions.

In truth, these caricatures of both the butterfly and spider ignore one important fact: either one may, in truth, be a line manager. In fact, the "boundary manager" of the future (and the present) needs some of these skills, whether he has a helpful, supportive outlook or a curious, wide-ranging one. Chief executives, though ostensibly power figures, are to some extent butterflies, picking up pictures of the outside world and then disseminating them within their organizations. The single-minded missionary of a particular technique or management package may really operate as a spider, assiduously building a de facto network of everyone who has shown any interest in his one true solution to the problems of the world, keeping them in touch with one another in order to reinforce the faith. A researcher or a secretary or a teacher or a consultant might operate in either mode.

One large company in the food industry has spent a number of years and a considerable sum of money trying to build into its management culture the basic tenet of the butterfly and spider creed: unlike money, with information, the more you give away, the more you get. This is particularly true of the informal information that oils the wheels of organizations as well as networks. In this case the company mounted a four-year training program starting with the board of directors and working out to every foreman to get across the idea that a manager's job was not to hoard information but to interpret it, to pass it up and down and around, translating it into the language of his listeners and illustrating his information with examples of how it might affect them. It was a slow process and difficult to measure, but my impression is that the company seems a more open place today.

With all the training in the world, neither spiders nor butterflies in their purest forms can be made. I believe some people are born with antennae that are a little more finely tuned, or instilled very early with attitudes that make it possible to work without power, even in organizations that value it highly. For these creatures, the motto "knowledge is power" has been replaced with:

Information is involvement.

Chapter 13.

TASK FORCES AND PROJECT TEAMS

In 1968 a book called *The Temporary Society* first pointed out the need for organizations that were not cast in concrete. The examples are more familiar to most of us today after several decades of big-is-beautiful excesses: the defensive "rule-book" reactions that set in when members of an organization realize its initial purpose is no longer primary; the diversions of the edifice complex or magic ratios or power games; the dwindling self-esteem as livelier members depart a no-longer-necessary group.

As the eighties and nineties loom, the need for temporary organizations becomes even more apparent. We need not simply "self-destruct mechanisms" but more, organizations or teams or groups that realize from their inception that they are temporary, so their entire behavior can be based on this awareness. We need them for positive reasons: to get things done efficiently. And we also need them as a mechanism to help permanent organizations change more rapidly.

Project teams existed with considerable verve in the early days of the aerospace and computer industries. I remember one group in a trailer-office in the parking lot of the Aerospace Corporation that put together in about six weeks the entire design and plan for a major missile. During this span the team members were completely turned on, caught up in the project to the exclusion of forms-filling-in, of regular lunch hours or coffee breaks, of evenings and weekends. The creative interaction and the shared sense of purpose welded them together for the span of the task; when the initial design was over, each member went back to his home department to pick up the threads of his normal work.

A few years later I watched for a few weeks as a similar group on the second floor of a rented building in Santa Monica argued over a blackboard as it evolved the design of the Sigma series of computers. Almost everyone in industry can point to some example, usually at the earliest stages of a new product, where project teams formed, welded, argued, created, and then dissolved, leaving among the members a wistful or nostalgic memory of the excitement, though they quickly forget the concomitant exhaustion.

Projects can be both fun and fruitful. But what is a "project"? So long as the connotation of a temporary system is there, it can mean just about anything you want it to mean:

* A project can be something that needs doing.

* A project can be something that needs learning about.

* A project can be a medium for two groups to get to know each other better.

* A project can be an excuse to try out a reorganization idea without first casting it in concrete.

* A project can be a vehicle for management development.

* A project can be a window to the outside.

* A project can inject new vitality into lackluster careers.

A project can also be dangerous. If it deals with the underlying assumptions or culture of the organization, and members of a project team begin to go around asking simple questions about these assumptions, people may feel the status quo is threatened. A project can raise political issues that cannot be resolved at the level of the project. A project can also raise the expectations of members of a project team, and if the organization does nothing about their plans, designs, or recommendations, the turned-on members will be far more skeptical and turned off afterwards than they were before they started. (A project can also be a conscious or unconscious exit or dehiring vehicle if it involves lots of outside fact-finding.)

A management development technique called "action learning" depends on projects, with participants organized in four- to six-man (or woman) "project sets." The technique seems effective and there are some aspects of its project teams that could be borrowed for other purposes, or grafted onto existing task forces and committees.

The size is, first of all, tidy. Five or six people working together seems to be an optimum number. (More than a dozen is usually too big.) The ancient universities had bedrooms for about five or six people on each staircase, sharing community rooms and facilities. This was presumed to be the ideal learning unit. Today most of the group work I've seen tends to rest on elements of a dozen or less, and those who have explored the phenomenon in some depth tend to break down their dozens into two sixes or three fours.

One important aspect of a project set is the ease and speed with which its members weld together. In action learning, each member usually works on a project of his own, and they report to one another for a full day every week or two. (The welding seems to be more effective and faster if they gather the night before for supper and informal talk, before going into their meetings the next day—a principle that probably holds for most other group activities as well, especially among people who are relatively new to one another.) Thus, the original model does not have a shared project, normally, to help the group weld. It still does so, with marvelous rapidity, so long as three conditions are met:

* The members have a long enough time with one another at the beginning to break through the social barriers.
* They regard one another as peers.
* They respect one another's projects.

Action learning is usually started because of management development or organizational development needs, but it turns out to be equally effective as a problem-solving or project-accomplishing mechanism. It doesn't matter whether the balance is more on management development or problem-solving, so long as there is progress on both fronts. And the results in action-learning are usually impressive. This, I believe, is mainly because the members of a project set motivate each other so strongly—just as the designers in their trailer on the back lot. Once a group welds and the members care about one another's problems along the way or their progress toward a joint objective, there is tremendous warmth —and drive—and concern in the questions they ask each other, the helpful suggestions, the co-consulting they give one another. Because this approach eliminates the teacher/student or boss/subordinate flavor, the members feel like adults and try very hard to live up to one another's expectations. It seems to be one of the approaches that focuses random activity into useful energy.

Another aspect of the project team or task force within an organization is the informal way it enriches the corporate bloodstream.

In one rather large company, membership in task forces is usually a kind of reward; a long history of projects and task force assignments has led to rich interconnections by which information flows naturally and easily, without regard to organizational or geographical barriers. So as soon as a problem occurs, a task force is pulled together, and already its members feel appreciated because they have been selected.

Top management blessings have been demonstrated

over previous projects, so people can take that important aspect for granted. In this company, task forces often have "subpoena power" to go fact-finding anywhere in the company (or outside) they think they can find pertinent information, so they have a strong sense of legitimacy. The assignments to task forces are usually full time for the short periods of their existence (at most a few months, but often only a few days) so the task forces don't suffer the split priorities of those who try to sandwich in an extra activity with their normal work loads. (When a member of a group is selected for a task force, the entire group usually feels honored and closes ranks to cover his normal job while he's away.) Because previous task forces are known throughout the company, and major changes are often identified by the name of the pertinent task-force leader, everyone expects the result of the effort to be action, as well as a report; therefore, a task force report usually gives rise to action, and the credibility of the mechanism increases yet again.

It's a win/win game, once you build a knowledge of task forces or project teams into the organization's memory and beliefs. Getting started is more difficult if an organization has not previously used temporary systems. Those who want to initiate a task force must first of all explain what it is, quite widely (because task forces and project teams usually need to do fact-finding on a fairly wide basis), and then emphasize its temporary nature as well as its importance. The best way to explain its importance is to assign to the pioneer task forces the best people suited to the tasks—people who are recognized in the organization not for their status but for their merit. If they return to jobs that are seen to be somewhat enriched, it also helps root the mechanism in the corporate culture, as with any other new mechanism.

Whether we call these "task forces" (which has a slightly military connotation to me and perhaps would tend to operate more hierarchically as a result) or "project teams" (which keeps the emphasis on the project rather than the force) or any other name that suits the organization, the principle is similar: to focus on something that needs doing, and in the process develop links among members and add flexibility to the organization; then, when the task is complete, to disband the temporary system as its members revert to their previous jobs. (Project teams and task forces are also useful places to stash people who are en route to new jobs.)

There are certain corporate cultures that set great store by immediate, measurable results, sometimes to their own discomfort. What happens in this environment if a project team should be "unsuccessful" in meeting the stated goal? Logically, if one wanted to encourage the use of project teams, there should be criteria for success, and thus (remembering yin and yang) there should be knowledge of failure. But remembering also that one byproduct of a project team is the development and learning of its individual members (unless this is the primary product and the project is a byproduct), it might be useful to treat the failure gently and explore instead what the members learned that would be useful to future project teams, or others endeavoring to work on similar problems. "The operation was a failure, but the surgeon learned a bit more about brain transplants."

How much power does a project team need? I think they work more by persuasion, by the visible commitment of their members, and by clarification, than they do by power. It is certainly important to have close links to power figures, who can hold lifelines out to a project team if it has turned over uncomfortable logs in the corporate jungle (or bail it out, or hold umbrellas over it, to mix metaphors still further). It makes sense to have a clear public announcement of a project team's formation (unless it is working on a secret new product), or to empower it to have access to any information it thinks will help.

Project team results are certainly likely to be more effective if it is a full-time rather than a part-time activity. If part-time approaches are necessary, it is better to cluster them in several days a week, rather than a few hours a day. And physical separation from the normal tasks will enhance the process. Full time or part time, it helps to have a residential period at the beginning, preferably with higher executives who are involved in the project or problem, to help teams weld together and thrash out what is expected of them.

I recognize that in this best of all possible worlds it is not always practical to assign people full time to projects, and there have been excellent projects that were haphazardly part time at best. In one company with twelve thousand employees, a new management development program has been slipped between everyone's ribs under the name of "projects," with no fanfare at all. Teams of four people from four different divisions are assigned to work part time for a few months on a problem belonging to someone in a fifth division. Members are selected for their specialist knowledge, but they are specialists who are worth developing toward generalist roles.

These projects start with a two-day get-together, including the sponsor in the host division, plus an outsider and a man from the personnel department, as "catalysts" to get things going, help define the problem, and help members begin to spell out the resources available and the routes for information, influence, and so on. Then they gather (starting the night before) about one day a month to report progress, with frequent phoning in between. One problem, for example, was the production, marketing, and viability of a proposed new product in the environmental field; after the project report, the product went into production, and as it succeeded, people began to pay more attention to the projects. Another project team investigated the use of trucks in an engineering subsidiary that was spending about $1 million a year on transport, and its recommendations saved about 10 percent of the cost. Gradually, organically, the company had a lively new form of management development or problem-solving, without ever having to make a commitment to the idea, beyond supporting each project.

Another approach for time-starved people gives some of

the merits of projects—an outside view, a sense of working with a peer, and focus on a problem or task—at virtually no cost to the organization. This might be termed "co-consulting," though it flies under many fancier names. In essence, people are formally or informally encouraged to pair off and spend some time trying to describe their problems to someone from another organization, or another part of the same organization. This forces you to organize your information and distill it, to take stock of where you really stand, and to answer seemingly simple-minded questions (such as "Why does your boss object to hiring a part-time clerk to handle that?"). If A spends half an hour telling his story to B, he then pays for the consulting assistance by sitting still himself for the next half hour and listening to B's situation. It is important to use the clock (anything from ten minutes up, but fairly measured, and in equal quantities), and it is important that the listener shut up, except to ask questions, until the last few minutes. One further benefit of this approach is that it gives some training in consultancy skills (by which I mean good listening—which is also a human skill and a management skill worthy of development). Although simple, the technique is surprisingly effective, even in fifteen-minute batches among people who have never seen one another before. It is especially well suited to members of a professional body, network, or any other kind of gathering of peers, not necessarily within the walls of their own organizations. But it does not give the team-membership benefits of real projects.

It's difficult for individual members of a part-time project team, because they seldom have any relief from the demands of their normal jobs. For these kinds of projects, a residential start is even more important. Another approach that can help is to set aside specific days when they are expected to be away from their offices working on the project, together or separately. The farther removed they are from normal phones and interruptions, the more humane the part-time project is likely to be.

Chapter 14.

AUTONOMOUS GROUPS

The welding together of a working group, temporary or permanent, is a curious process, quite similar to individual growth. It involves growing confidence, expanding horizons, shared achievement, and enough time spent together in both formal and informal activities to build trust, shared confidence, and a sense of how the various members fit together.

Sometimes the term "autonomous groups" conjures up pictures of automatons, performing with robotlike efficiency in some "Modern Times" type factory. The reverse is, or ought to be, the case: an individual operating inside a group with some autonomy ought to have a greater sense of controlling his own world.

Henry Boettinger, recently in organization and strategic work at AT&T, has an interesting set of observations, gleaned from one of the world's largest organizations, that apply to many others. He says:

* Any organization can be made to work.

* The more the members design it, the better it's likely to work.

* The members (and outsiders) need to know the criteria by which their success will be measured. What is the task?

* Different problems or organizations demand different personalities.

* Different personalities demand different organizational types.

* If the criteria for success are explicit, a group can be autonomous.

* Look for games where everybody wins.

To gain confidence and a sense of its own legitimacy, a group needs many of the same things an individual needs. My experience observing autonomous working groups, especially in Sweden, indicates certain elements that can speed the growth of a group's self-image:

* *Visible achievement.* When a group can point to last week's record output or a report that has taken the eye of the president or an important deadline met, members share something special with one another and like to hear about the achievement from outsiders.

* *Clear boundaries.* Whether it's physical, geographical, political, or emotional, the group needs to know how much room it has in which to operate with minimum interference.

* *More autonomy within them.* Even if the boundaries remain the same, the sense of being a group can be enhanced by making sure the group is subjected to no interference within its span of responsibility.

* *Self-help skills.* This is something that autonomous groups seem to develop for themselves once they begin to weld together and gain some sense of their own legitimacy. In Volvo, when pay was deemed to depend on the number of different jobs an employee could do, the more autonomous groups rapidly taught one another an astonishing number of jobs to maximize the income of each member who wanted to learn other tasks. No formal training program was

necessary, and the jobs were learned just as competently as in formal programs.

* *Resources to grow.* Just as an individual who has done well at a task wants to be rewarded with a new task, so it is with some autonomous groups. "Growth" is harder to arrange (once a group is welded it doesn't usually want to change its number or place on the organization chart) but worth the effort if the learning of the group can continue and be seen to be a reward.

* *Minimum bureaucracy.* Good working groups are usually impatient with "them," people at the center or staff types or any other intruding purveyor of policies and reasons it can't do things the way it wants to. The fewer restrictions a well-welded group has, the more likely it is to be productive.

* *Reliable information.* This means information the group members rely on, not formal information that is 100 percent guaranteed to be correct. It can help the group if the formal information system includes good feedback on the group's performance (as with the quality control systems in the Volvo Kalmar factory), which can remind any working group, e.g. through a computer terminal, what it did to fix a particular problem the last time it happened). Mainly, good data is "G-2," informal intelligence about the quality or quantity of items coming into the group or problems the next group has had with its output or the real dope about the proposed reorganization and where they think they're going to move us to.

* *Maximum confidence.* Once a group has achieved something together, confidence begins to grow; it can be nurtured if higher management takes public notice of achievement.

One small technique to help groups achieve a sense of their own existence is overlooked in many shop-floor situations. The facilities budget, for maintenance and upkeep and painting the bathrooms and buying new lights and so on is usually controlled, quite unnecessarily, by facilities experts. I have seldom found any good reason for this to be so. Whatever they do, the experts can't do as good a job of deciding what color the walls should be or the toilets or what kind of lighting or Muzak to have, as could a group that has to live in the area. It costs no more to break out the facilities budget and let groups spend it as they will; it might look funny to have a factory that was passion pink in one section, cool blue in another, and unpainted but with super lighting in a third area—but that's not necessarily a bad thing.

It's like giving a clothes allowance to a twelve-year-old daughter; she may spend all of it on jeans for six months to the exclusion of socks, shirts, and sweaters, but eventually she'll have more confidence in her own ability to make decisions, and the decisions themselves will grow more balanced. And the sooner she starts, the less the mistakes are likely to cost her (or you). So with groups, the first joint ventures into spending money together will be tentative, and any negative reaction from central or higher management will send the tendrils of confidence back into their protective solitude: "I knew they didn't really mean it."

At Volvo they carried this approach to surprising lengths. In the mile-long Torslanda factory, which had been built before the days of autonomous group working, four major areas were identified and each handled separately from a facilities viewpoint. The body group commissioned the local architectural college to come help it design its area, and models of the proposals were put on view for several weeks for all the employees in the body area. The result was bright, and most people were pleased; eventually, other groups competed in modern designs. In another area, about twenty assemblers had a roof installed over their part of the line. Ostensibly for lighting and noise control, the little roof actually denoted their working area and increased the sense of belonging to a specific group.

They used to say that the family that prays together stays together. I would propose that the group that plays together stays together. People would say that in many situations it isn't possible to socialize outside working hours; if that's actually the case, then a group might as well have some legitimate social time *inside* working hours. Almost any manager whose group has experienced residential training or other outside activities together can testify to the morale, productivity, and group-welding benefits of time spent together outside the normal work context.

Eight Characters in Search of a Committee

I recently resigned from an executive committee because I felt my contributions had been less than helpful and were in danger of being divisive. I felt guilty and "failed" because the group's objective was one I shared. My office-mate asked me about the personalities of the other members. After I told him about a few meetings, he smiled: "That wasn't your fault. The committee just didn't have the right mix of members." He then gave me a little test that absolved my guilts: nobody could score high on all eight types of committee roles—and committees or working groups usually need most of the skills in the list. The winning team contains all the elements and uses them well.

Belbin's team at Cambridge evolved this list of team roles, based on work in management games. They found, incidentally, that teams with slightly lower averages on creative and analytical skills usually did quite well; what was critical was the breadth or range of these skills within a single team. The Ideas Man needs a gap in creativity between himself and the others. Such a team may have more respect for the social aspects of team membership, the yin or right-hemisphere elements, and are more conscious of their roles, rather than focusing sharply and rationally on the expertise of members in specific functions. Teams that were functionally organized usually worked smoothly until something unpredictable changed the ground rules, and then it became clear they really weren't teams at all, just collections of specialists.

Belbin's people also found that even if you get the right mix of members, based on the types listed below, they don't always use themselves in the right ways. This leads to the notion that improvements can be brought about in most management teams by analyzing not only the task or functional roles of the various members but also the team-member roles. To some extent each individual has particular roles that are natural, but one person might be able to play one of several roles, given a little opportunity to think about the social composition of the team. The balance of a team can thus be adjusted either by changing one or more of the individuals in it, or by encouraging certain individuals to play a different team role; in either case, improvements have been consistent and impressive.

Seven of the eight types listed below are needed in a team. The "Chairman" and "Shaper" roles, though quite different, are (or should be) mutually exclusive. If you have a chairman, you don't want a shaper, and vice versa. The other roles can be shared out, as long as balance is maintained, in any group from five to about a dozen. Incidentally, there are elaborate personality tests to identify individual characteristics, once people have had a chance to discuss these team roles; but I think most are quite accurate in assessing themselves and their fellow members as to which roles they fit, without any further testing or evaluation from on high or outside.

1. *The Chairman.* He might also be termed "the coordinator." He likes organizing people, mapping their strengths, and using them productively. He

engineers consent and develops agreement among different interests. He commands respect and inspires enthusiasm, has a sense of timing and balance, and communicates easily. He doesn't necessarily have to be a ball of fire on the creative or intellectual front.

2. *The Shaper.* This is the one I'd call "the fearless father figure." He's the forceful type who likes to influence group decisions, to make his mark in meetings. He's willing to risk unpopularity to get his ideas across to the group and usually directs his attention to setting objectives and priorities and making sure the group's discussion and action take on the right shape or pattern. His drive and self-confidence are likely to be balanced by an intolerance toward vague ideas and people.

3. *The Contacts Man.* This is my "butterfly," flitting around the boundaries. He often looks farther afield than the immediate task and brings in ideas, developments, and phone numbers from outside. He works by personal networks and contacts, likes new ideas and techniques. He can usually find the right specialist to help at a moment's notice and he works well by telephone. He is likely to have an outgoing, relaxed personality, strong on curiosity and willing to see the possibilities in anything new. Conversely, he may suffer from overenthusiasm or a lack of follow-up.

4. *The Ideas Man.* This is the "innovator," the original, independent, imaginative cuss, who is often frustrated in group work. He's a source of new approaches to old problems and new ideas and strategies to tackle. He likes puzzles, patterns, and problem-solving and is probably valued for his independent outlook as well as his intelligence and

/ *145*

imagination. His tolerable weaknesses probably include a tendency to be impractical on occasion or weakness at communicating his ideas to members with different outlooks and attitudes.

5. *The Critic.* You might call him "the analyst." He's the careful, critical member, often slow but right. His judgment wins over his feelings, and his contributions are analyzing problems and evaluating other people's ideas and suggestions. He can poke holes in unsound proposals (sometimes quite early) and make sure all the information is on hand before a decision is made. He's long on critical thinking and objectivity but he probably tends to be over-serious, unexciting, and overcritical on occasion. At the creative stage of problem-solving it's probably best to send him away to do something useful elsewhere.

6. *The Implementer.* He's the practical type who sticks to it, meeting targets and deadlines. He wants clear objectives and procedures and is sometimes uncomfortable with new ideas. He's the solid, systematic member who will make a practical plan to achieve the objective when the others have finished arguing about it. The implementer is necessary—nay, crucial —for turning concepts and plans into practical working procedures and for carrying out agreed plans systematically. His strengths include self-control and self-discipline as well as realism and practical common sense. He may be a trifle inflexible and unresponsive to unproven new ideas.

7. *The Team-Builder.* If the shaper is a fearless father figure, then this is the nurturing mother figure. He likes people and works easily with them, even when their ideas differ from his own. He'll support the others in their strengths and underpin their weak-

nesses, while he oils the communications machinery among them. His strengths include humility, flexibility, popularity, and listening skills—but they may be offset by a lack of decisiveness or toughness and a distaste for competition and friction among his team members.

8. *The Inspector.* While the ideas man or the butterfly starts things, the inspector is the one who finishes them. This is the one I call "the perfectionist" because he's the one most likely to notice omissions and mistakes, with his fine eye for detail. His role is to make sure the team is protected from errors of commission and omission and keeping track of the portions of the task that need extra attention. He also maintains a sense of urgency in the team, acting as its conscience. If there aren't enough current problems to worry about, he may be forced to create anxiety about possible future problems. His strengths include a strong sense of order and purpose, a sense of concern, plus self-control and strength of character. His foibles are likely to include impatience, an inability to suffer fools gladly, and intolerance toward members who have more casual habits and dispositions.

The group in which I felt unsuccessful actually had two chairmen (or a chairman and a shaper) and no inspector, so my original ideas and contacts were seldom helpful. Many groups that don't quite seem to click may simply be suffering from absence of one of these elements, or a lack of clarity among the members about their own innate styles as well as their formal roles in the group or committee.

There is tremendous energy in a group, as anyone knows who has ever enjoyed a stint in a creative, productive group. (The two are not always synonymous, but when they are, it's a splendid experience.) People go to work and pour their energy into the task, not for the formal pay or rewards nearly so much as for the shared experience, the exhilaration of achieving something worthwhile with people who have become very close.

In one Swedish working group I heard about a member who had been taking somewhat more than his share of sick leave. In a voice that no manager could ever wield, fellow workers telephoned the layabout and said, in essence: "See here, Peter, if you don't get in here by two o'clock there's going to be hell to pay. We're behind schedule as it is and you're not carrying your weight." He was there at 1:30.

Leading a Group

The manager of a working group (by which I obviously mean an intimate ten- to twelve-man "hunting band" as Antony Jay would call it) works almost entirely by personal credibility. The group is too small an element to respond successfully to power; even so, I have known many group leaders who were natural autocrats, though their right to govern stemmed from being right rather than from being "governor" (or "guv," the British slang term for "boss").

There have been many experiments with leaderless work groups, and any group whose leader is away works in this manner; I think experience has shown that in a small working group, the members know who has what kind of know-how, judgment, or skill and usually turn to the appropriate member. Most work groups in China are leaderless and co-ordination tasks as well as monitoring are usually shared among members.

There have been disastrous consequences in small groups when a perfectly useful member who does not have management skill or confidence is thrust into a position of leadership, without the consent of the governed, and tries to enforce his will on the group in which he was formerly a member. The result of such appointments is often a rapid slide into power politics and tiny factions, with drastic effects on overall productivity. The damage to the individual who tried to manage and failed can also be considerable. Once he has seen himself in the higher position, it is difficult to contemplate demotion; he may cling to the illusions of managing much too long (which encourages the behavior enshrined in *The Peter Principle*), or he may come to view himself as a failure when he was really a success at his pre-manager role. Technical firms in the computer and aerospace industries are peppered with tragic figures who were rewarded for being good engineers by promotions into management when their only training was coping on the job, and their only mentors were other good engineers who had been rewarded earlier. Being able to do the job better than the troops do it is *not* the essence of good management, and such managers (including some who have developed themselves quite competently) tend to overmanage.

Once team roles have sorted themselves out, most working groups thrive on the least management possible and the most autonomy consistent with what they are expected to produce. If it is ideas, leave them almost completely alone; if it is thirty radios a day, let them schedule their own breaks as much as possible.

One way around the leadership conundrum for a close-knit group that loses its natural head or chairman or shaper is to appoint a member as contact man to the outside. If he views his role as public relations and fact-finding, in line with the team roles, rather than trying to manage the group, his expectations and those of the group are more likely to be met. A chairman or shaper *is* necessary, but a group can get along internally without one for a surprisingly long time if necessary, while it cannot go without the linkage portion of the leader's role.

Chapter 15.

CORPORATE CULTURES

When sociologists or anthropologists refer to the unique characteristics of a nation or tribe, they talk about its "culture." When psychologists talk about similar characteristics of an individual, they talk about "personality." We don't really have a commonly accepted term for these characteristics as they refer to a working organization, but I am going to borrow the term "culture" because most people know what it means, in general terms.

The culture of an organization, though, is like the personality of an individual in that it stems from early experiences, "genetic" factors in the sense of the sort of people it attracts and holds (they might be analogous to the elements in the DNA coding that determines a person's physical characteristics), and a kind of mythology that builds up, a set of models by which that organization operates and sees the world around it.

Heroes and Villains

Like the culture of a tribe, a corporate culture is an amalgam of the heroes and villains, of the commandments, of the crimes and punishments, of all the oral mythology that permeates the tribe. You can get fired for putting in expense accounts that are too high—or you can get fired for putting in expense accounts that are too low. "You can get fired for . . ." is one way the culture manifests itself, because banishment from the tribe is the ultimate punishment, a kind of corporate execution.

Another manifestation of culture is the way you can get ahead. Here you wear a necktie and carry a briefcase; there you arrive in tennis shoes and talk about golf. I know several UK firms where Management By Motor operates—status judged by the engine size of the company car. In one electronics company every aspiring young executive joined the Jaycees and the Young Republicans, no matter what. The founders believed in helping the community that had helped them get started; the next level of management took part in a wide variety of community activities. By the time you got three or four levels down, the forms of community service were highly stylized, and the idea of community service had lost itself in anxiety about whether one would win the election to be Jaycee secretary or not.

The founders of that company didn't set out to create a tribe of Jaycees and Young Republicans. It happened of its own accord as their actions were copied, and beliefs about their beliefs spread.

It is possible to turn this phenomenon to useful account, to "create" a new element in a corporate culture, but it can only be done through the informal machinery, the eyes of the beholders. One company that wanted to create management vacancies at a time of very slow growth started a program to encourage middle managers to look outside in the community for tasks that needed doing, and apply for one-year or six-month assignments at company expense to do them. The first few people to do this (with personal encouragement from key executives) were exceptionally able managers, well regarded by everyone else. When they came back from their outside assignments they were seen to go into interesting new jobs, in several cases a notch up the corporate ladder. After that the company had no trouble getting managers to move out into the community, even though a clogged-up management structure would normally have reacted with fear, and individuals would not normally want to suffer being out of sight, out of mind during perilous times. Because the company built outside assignments into the management culture, it was able to create "holes" and use them as development jobs; thus, it could maintain a slightly larger and better-than-average pool of turned-on managers through the difficult period. Even when times improved, the outside assignments continued, improving the company's connections to the community.

A sublime unawareness of corporate cultures seems particularly rooted in the Western tradition. Pascale writes:

> The Japanese distinguish between our notion of "organization" and their notion of "the company." In their minds, the term organization refers only to the system; their concept of the company includes its underlying character as well. A company's character describes a shared sense of values long held by members and enforced by group norms. The result is an institutional way of doing things that is different from what efficiency alone would require. The "company" may accomplish the same tasks as an "organization" does, but it occupies more space, moves with more weight, and reflects a commitment to larger ends than just the accomplishment of a mission.

I would contend that this is true, de facto, even in companies that don't recognize and augment their own cultures. Incidentally, Pascale studied Japanese companies operating in the United States; these spent three times as much money on social and recreational facilities for their employees as did their American counterparts ($48.85 per employee, versus $14.85 for the American companies). Pascale says: "Some of these programs were probably largely symbolic, but many also fostered increased off-the-job contact among employees. Their benefit was to 'personalize' the particular company."

The Organizational Subconscious

Very little has been done to study the contribution of its culture to the effectiveness of an organization. Perhaps because we have been so completely enmeshed in the formal, logical, left-hemisphere elements of organizations for several decades, we tend to overlook the existence of this underlying, right-hemisphere aspect. Yet just as a person will be less effective if he is forced to behave in ways that are not natural for his personality, so it is with organizations. Policies and plans that don't really fit the underlying culture will not work as well as those that do.

It can take an individual years of analysis (self or psychiatric) to come to terms with his own personality. Just imagine how much more complex the task is to come to terms with organizational cultures. I spent three years studying the history of a single company, and when I finished I had still only begun to scratch the surface. On the other hand, the knowledge I gathered of its innate patterns is still useful in predicting how that company will behave, so the effort is undoubtedly worthwhile.

It is very difficult for people inside an organization to analyze its culture, especially if they have spent most of their working lives in that one organization. Similarly, it is difficult for an individual, unaided, to analyze his own personality, though we all try most of the time. The view from outside is helpful in one way or another. And the view into another organization can often offer insights into one's own that are surprising and helpful.

One expert who studies organizations found what may be a slight shortcut to capturing some kind of vignette of a corporate culture. Whenever he is invited into a company (usually to help it change its behavior in some way), he starts out by saying: "Of course I'll have to generate a company history first." The chairman nods happily and is then surprised to come into his boardroom the following Monday and find half a dozen of the gold-watch brigade, retired employees from various elements and stages of the company's development, gathered with coffee cups, talking to the expert and his tape machine. The well-chosen retired people spend a few days reliving olden times. When they finish, the expert writes up a short, behaviorally oriented report, encapsulating the company's history.

When he finishes his history, he calmly tells the chairman it will now be published for all the employees, to serve as a start-point in the change program. If the chairman flinches, stamps "secret" all over it, and locks it up in the corporate safe, the expert departs for greener pastures. If the chairman is willing to discuss and publish the history, the expert has some kind of shared perception of the culture with which to begin discussing current aspects of the corporate behavior patterns.

Per-Olof Berg studied the history of one Swedish company in the form of sixty-one little "dramas" that had cropped up in everyone's telling. It might be a downturn in the market or the arrival of a new personnel director or the completion of a new building, but some event takes on meaning beyond its seeming importance. Berg, incidentally, spent quite a lot of time identifying "key informants" and "key actors." He found out that the worst-informed key informant was much better informed than the best-informed key actor—an observation supported by my own years of corporate research. Some people are simply good observers; the actors are usually so busy in the here-and-now politics of their situations that they don't see as many useful details or overall patterns of behavior. (One more "thinking" and "doing" dichotomy.)

The culture isn't just something for corporate historians to file away. This interaction of past history with present behavior is the one valid reason I see to delve into the events that lurk in a corporate backbone. I remember one chief executive to whom I had sent a fairly lurid description of his corporation's attempts to keep the nosy press out of affairs that were mainly to its credit. When we discussed my access problems, he said: "You know, that portcullis probably came down in 1966, when I got so mad after a couple of big articles about the company. When I sneeze the Dallas office tends to explode." In his case, the early articles (also harmless but irritating because they contained lively quotes from senior executives) had been the starting point for a public relations department that became the watchdogs, preventing any more bad press. As time went on they did their job well —to the extent that they prevented a lot of good press, too, and eventually the company was so closed off that many people assumed it must have secrets to hide if it was so concerned about keeping the press controlled. The reaction to a 1966 "sneeze" was a 1976 neurosis that did the company more harm than good. Dismantling all the carefully built machinery will probably take until 1986, if it can be done at all.

Small Events Cast Long Shadows

Another small incident reveals how deep into the behavior or language of its members an event in the corporate culture can go. I began to be curious when three different managers in a large oil company, from different portions, at different times, objected to the word "manager." I finally asked one of them: "How do you identify yourself on your passport?" "Oil company executive," he answered. The next time I met a manager from that company I asked him the same question, and he answered: "Agronomist." Finally, one day in the executive bar, I met two retired finance men and I asked them, too. They were both "oil company executives."

"What's wrong with the word 'manager'?" I asked.

The first said: "I don't know; I just don't like the sound of it."

The second looked off into the distance for a moment and then said: "Doesn't that go back to that government ruling for a little while in the fifties? As I remember, if we 'managed' a foreign subsidiary, we had to incorporate its revenues in our accounts. So overnight, a lot of 'managers' became 'coordinators' or 'administrators' or 'executives,' and I think it was about then that the word 'manager' started to disappear from our vocabulary."

To this day, young tigers in the company quickly learn to aspire to the exalted title of "coordinator."

Small incidents that have long, and sometimes large, effects—those are the roots of the corporate culture. (Those are the roots of an individual's personality, too, I suppose.) Occasionally, if they are counterproductive, it can be useful to dig them out and examine them. More often, though, simply understanding the general outlook or framework of corporate culture in its current form is all that people need to work with it.

One important element in the culture is the kinds of people the organization hires and promotes. A model usually develops. You can tell a Shell man from a Raytheon man from a Honeywell man almost at first glance. It isn't always true that the progenitor hires everyone in his own image (the "doppelganger effect," as Bennis once called it), but there is in most large, established companies a tendency for certain types of people to get ahead faster, aside from merit.

Some companies hire people right from college and train them in the corporate model; they are likely to have quite coherent cultures, with values shared throughout the organization, largely unquestioned. Other companies take their managers on an easy-come, easy-go basis, head-hunting from other companies when openings have to be filled. These tend to have less identifiable cultures, though certain types of behavior or personality will prevail no matter what other corporate origins their bearers have; such companies are also likely to have identifiable subcultures, pockets where one strong leader, no matter where he came from, has built up a group of his own people, who tend to move around within the organization as he moves (or outside it, for that matter).

Take the computer industry. IBM might be termed a "family"-oriented company, with highly motivated young people flowing into the company, usually straight from college, and absorbing its values and ethics, which are clearly spelled out and extend far beyond normal business practice. IBM is socially responsible, very care-taking of its employees, and generally behaves as if it believed it would still be the industry leader whatever the industry becomes in one hundred years' time.

I worked for another computer company once that might be termed a "sexy" company. The founder liked pulchritude and surrounded himself with executives who also thrived in the zestful environment he created—with perhaps an overabundance of pneumatic secretaries in the early days. It was the kind of company where people came and went rapidly, never dull, not always orderly, but highly creative, especially in its early days. Eventually, as computer companies were merging all over the landscape, it was taken over by a much more orderly company, but the two never quite understood each other, and the merger never quite jelled.

Burroughs, seen from outside, had a culture I would term "creative high-technology," with more quirky people and ideas than average, somewhat underpromoted and underappreciated outside. NCR's culture dated back to the early days of cash registers; even twenty years into the computer era it has a strong marketing flavor but the marketeers seem dominated by the kind of thinking that won NCR a place in history for big, beautiful, mechanical machines. (You still find ancient NCR cash registers in antique shops today.) I think of Univac as a "traditional" culture in computer industry terms, with big-machine overtones, no matter how small the new machines they sell. Honeywell has had several mergers of unmatched corporate cultures, East and West Coast people and machines, but an East Coast flavor prevails, overlaid by a high-technology flavor inherited from GE.

These are just outsider sketches, but they may help demonstrate how cultures are seen and judged from outside. And just as people will choose to associate with individuals who are "like me," so companies tend to judge other companies and associate with them for reasons of cultural empathy as much as practical or logical matching. In most "social responsibility" or "community support" campaigns you find key people from the same five or six companies leading the pack, just as you find another five or six firms involved in anything to do with sport, and a slightly different mix offering patronage to ballet, opera, theaters, and art exhibits. The art of grantsmanship in many semi-public or volunteer groups today amounts to knowing who, in each of these firms, has control of the good-works purse strings, and for which types of activities they will open. In this sense, the culture of the modern corporation is taking on a tinge of feudalism, with the corporation as patron of the arts. (It has also been pointed out that the last place where real servants exist, at least in Great Britain, is the executive suite; only there can you depend on having your tea or coffee impeccably served in sparkling china by a silent, superbly appointed secretary. For this, we are told to be grateful to the word processor that has liberated her from the drudgery of typing!)

Corporate cultures come to the fore most vividly in acquisitions and mergers. One European computer company suffered eight mergers among portions of fifteen predecessor companies. Even today, almost fifteen years since the last merger, you can find pockets in various locations (not always the same location where they started) who identify themselves as being from one of the predecessor companies. More important, the products they design and build, no matter how rational the corporate planning, still carry the hallmarks of those earlier companies and their cultures. So its little machines don't really fit as well with its big machines as, logically, they should. (The same is true of most other merged computer companies, so I'm not giving any trade secrets away.)

Because of cultural differences and human resistance to change, I think we could devise a rule of thumb:

Merger A doesn't take until merger B occurs
or management team C comes in.

Going back to the Honeywell example, the Massachusetts portion of the firm took over a West Coast computer company in the early sixties. The two co-existed for a few years without ever "merging" people, styles, or behavior patterns until Honeywell took over GE's Phoenix-based computer activities around 1970. Then the two preceding Honeywell elements tended to cluster together a little more (better the enemy you know . . .) to protect themselves from any possible incursions from the Phoenix newcomers. Both organizational upheavals actually worked fairly well, I think, because they were clear-cut "takeovers" rather than mergers. In the European example, though, there had been a number of mergers in which no one was quite sure who was on top, and the persistence of the early cultures continued unabated until an American was brought in as chief executive; he brought with him a number of key men, and for a while it looked as if all the earlier elements were united to beat off the Americans. Eventually, the Americans departed for America, leaving behind a nearly merged company ten years late.

Cultures would probably explain why the perfectly logical "economies of scale" and other fiscal reasons for the conglomerates of the sixties didn't live up to their promises. During a takeover or merger, a great deal of individual and group and organizational energy goes into protecting the status quo for the original living system. The formal plans never take into account the time and energy it requires to overcome resistance to change in this situation, or the persistence of tendencies to revert to the earlier ways. Remembering that the key actors are not usually key observers, it is easier to understand why people who are bringing about such mergers and takeovers are not likely to see cultural hurdles.

Today mergers are less important than the tendency for

organizations to "dis-merge" themselves, to dismantle large elements and break them down into more manageable, more autonomous, more "natural," and certainly smaller units. I sometimes worry that the dis-merging, like the merging that preceded it, seems to be rather firmly in the hands of the strategic types, the corporate planners and their ilk. But this is where an awareness of corporate cultures on the part of the doers as well as the thinkers and planners and observers could make a major difference. If the new elements are artificially gerrymandered across ancient cultural lines, they are less likely to be workable than those that observe natural cultural boundaries within the organization. Awareness of those boundaries is likely to be greater as you get closer to them.

What we will need to create, if this is the direction of our future, is a crop of corporate sociologists (by some other name) who can wander freely in a company, observing its boundaries and traditions, and helping the planners and change agents see and respect those boundaries and traditions, too. I don't think the traditional sociologists are equipped for this task, unless they can unlearn their expert terminology. It might be useful instead to create project teams to learn enough about sociology that they could bring some of its tools back to the company. It might also be useful to find managers with some sensitivity and communication skills and interest in corporate cultures, and then develop them by trading them into a different corporate culture for a while. These kinds of assignments are already occurring here and there, but they have not so far been pointed at developing skills in understanding corporate cultures.

Chapter 16.

MANAGING FROM OUTSIDE

The corporate culture is the key to managing or influencing an organization from outside as well as inside. If you understand that, you have a much better chance of attracting the attention of the people who can make things happen (or not happen).

In spite of the rising tides of consumerism and environmentalism—and the concomitant rise in corporate departments to buffer decision-makers from outsiders—there is nothing new in the basic approaches to organizations. More than twenty-five years ago my father, unhappy with a pair of ski boots, wrote a letter to the president of the family-owned manufacturing firm. He received a new pair of ski boots. I can think of perhaps a dozen battles with bureaucracy: tax assessors, insurance claims people, salespeople in department stores, or company administrators. If my idea of "fair" and their idea of protecting the organization were out of step with each other, I was made to feel powerless and dejected. Fortunately, in the face of this kind of corporate claustrophobia, I usually overreacted with outraged letters to the president, or reasonable facsimiles thereof, and I began to learn that companies and even government departments *could* be influenced, once you knew how. It usually takes information, time, energy, and limitless patience, so the goal has to be worth the investment (in both formal and informal terms); most organizations are susceptible to outside impulses.

Most outsiders trying to change corporate policies (or even get a pair of faulty boots changed) are irate. They feel they have been wronged, and it usually takes a measure of irritation to spur one to try to influence the organization anyway. So they write an angry letter to whomever it may concern. Whomever (probably a twenty-year-old clerk with only a few minutes to go before lunch) glances at it, puts it in category 2-D, and sends out a mimeographed "Sorry, but no" note, or these days gets the almighty word-processor to type out a snazzy, personalized "Sorry, but no, dear Mrs. Jones" letter.

So rule one in managing from outside is quite simple: *the angrier you are the sweeter should be your letters.*

The next step is to take matters out of the hands of the clerk, no matter how concerned you may be about trends in white-collar employment or jobs for young people, and move your issue upstairs into the executive suite. This is fairly easy once you know who lives there. And that can be ascertained by phoning the company or its local office. I usually identify myself and my organization (rather rapidly on occasion) and tell the switchboard girl that I've misplaced, or don't know, the names of the chairman and chief executive. Then I ask the name of the public relations director (and sometimes the vice president for personnel as well). Switchboard girls are usually excellent at getting the spelling right for names, titles, addresses, and extension numbers. I thank them effusively, then hang up.

From this point, with a complaint, for example, there are several approaches. One says tell the lower-down boys first, so you keep the top brass in reserve. The other says start at the top where you're most likely to find some joy. If you want something relatively minor (such as your VW valued for a few hundred dollars more when someone has smashed it), it's probably best to write to the director of public relations, noting your case in pleasant terms (two paragraphs will usually do) and suggesting that it's not good for the image of his company to be seen to be niggardly in such matters. The tone of communication should give him every reason to want to help a good consumer such as you.

If the response is form 2-D, personalized letter 2-D, or the version thereof signed by the director, then it's time to write him again, restating your case, referring to your earlier letter (which may have been destroyed), and sending a carbon copy to the chief executive. If once again there is no joy, the later stages can, again by carbon copy, invoke the attention of outside bodies who you believe will take an interest—the local paper, Ralph Nader, or the congressional inquiry into faulty ski boots. It's a funny thing, but the receipt of a letter which says demurely at the bottom: "cc: Charles Thompson" forces you to read the letter through the eyes of Thompson and to respond as if he were looking over your shoulder. Thus, whether Charles Thompson or Ralph Nader cares about the issue or not is less important than the niggling worry the recipient will have about the state of mind or sensitivity of Thompson, Nader, or whoever. This only works well, though, if you have bothered to get the names, titles, and internal relationships right.

Leverage?

As with employee relations, an issue that goes into a polarized, contentious framework becomes a lose/lose game. To win you need to develop the area of mutual interest, of cooperation. And this is often most easily done in informal ways. The individual may be powerless, but his well-reasoned letter to the president may receive just as much attention as the one that comes from a special-interest group with a thousand members. Indeed, if you are trying to convince a company that the times are changing and that its stream-polluting factory will have to change its ways, it will probably be more effective to orchestrate a campaign by which individuals write to various executives and members of the board of directors to enhance a sense of bandwagon than to have a single, visible environmental lobby point the finger of accusation. Individually, tones of voice that express "concern" can be effective in injecting more information into the organization, where the natural tendency to fight, grouping together for strength and leverage (and a cozy sense of membership), may close the shutters against such information.

It *is* important to muster visible numbers of people when you are trying to change a fairly major policy of an organization (especially if the change is obviously going to cost it money), but save the leverage for later. It may be most useful to use the numbers of people who share your interest as sources of information, ideas, and inspiration in the early stages. Who knows how the organization ticks? Does anyone have friends there? Who are their heroes and villains? What are they afraid of? This last bit of information is tempting to use right away. But think of the partners in a marriage; each knows how to hurt the other, but if the marriage is to be workable, the partners need that knowledge only in order to *avoid* hurting each other. Similarly, to manage an organization effectively from outside, you need to be very delicate about its collective ego. If someone has been at fault, try to sidestep the faultfinding and concentrate on remedy.

At the same time, one must muster one's forces. "Speak softly and carry a big stick," Teddy Roosevelt advised. In today's organizational world, publicity is certainly a big stick. So is regulation. So are injunctions and lawsuits and investigations. So are unions, sometimes. If your issue is worth the effort, it certainly helps to begin mapping the resources available in the media, the government, and other bodies. It is often more useful to drop a key name casually into a pleasant discussion than it is to threaten exposure to one of these fearsome outside bodies—the carbon-copy effect, writ somewhat larger.

Open Door to the Outside

A few years ago when I was doing research about IBM (somewhat contrary to the corporation's desire for privacy),

I began to learn a great deal about the "Open Door" policy by which any disgruntled employee could exercise the open door of any executive up the ladder if the employee believed he had been wronged in some way. Throughout sixty years and more of use the policy had been enshrined and institutionalized but it still worked. Employees *did* go see their boss' boss' boss if they felt he was the right man to right the wrong they had suffered. One interesting finding: there is very little abuse of such a system. People almost always go direct to the most effective level. The president's office is *not* cluttered up with disgruntled workers complaining about trivia—but the knowledge that people can go all the way to the top is a powerful incentive to managers lower down to solve the problems before they get out of hand.

The Open Door was effective in another way. Not only did employees feel they could get satisfaction, but also managers learned how to handle grievances early and well. Furthermore, they learned to document cases carefully if they believed an employee was likely to be unhappy about any decision. This kind of atmosphere takes time to build, but it works.

It also works from outside. Understanding the language and flavor of the internal policy, I could use it to get information, or to complain about those who were keeping me from getting information. Once in a while I could gain access through my self-bestowed Open Door to an executive who I believed could change some bit of corporate behavior for the better, or help some outside cause which I felt would fit the corporate self-image.

The employee uses the Open Door to right what he believes to be a wrong, but not simply for self-aggrandizement. Similarly, I don't think I could use my Open Door into the corporation for my own benefit. In the insurance instance, it was one thing to take umbrage when my poor VW was so insultingly undervalued; at some point, though, to keep writing would have approached unethical behavior, once my sense of "fairness" had been assuaged.

Not every company or government body has an Open Door policy, even inside. But it *is* possible to help them create one, informally, to the outside. And the ability to use their own language and values in dealing with your concern gives you a much better chance to influence people who are making decisions in the organization.

Chapter 17.

SELF-SUSTAINING ORGANIZATIONS

As the population of well-developed mobile managers increases, we're going to see an increasing number of projects and innovations that wither and die as they move. Already, if one of these managers is describing a project that turned him on, I have learned to ask: "What happened to it after you left?" The answer is usually mumbled, slightly troubled: "It ran on for a while but nobody really picked it up, and eventually I think it died."

One day, though, I ran into a man who was talking warmly about a scout troop he had once started for a group of handicapped children. "What happened when you left?" I intoned. "Oh, that was fifteen years ago, but it's still running well," he said. "Whenever I do something like that, I try to make it self-sustaining."

Individual Innovation and Group Ownership

His experience ought to be transferrable, if we are to encourage more mobility and more projects in the future. The secret, if such there be, was really quite simple: the innovation was his own, but instead of implementing it all himself —thus becoming essential to it, appreciated for it, and feeling slightly heroic—he involved other people sufficiently early that most of them ended up feeling it was really their idea. The manager got less credit, but the project had a better chance of surviving his departure.

The composition of a group, discussed in Chapter 14, may give us some clues as to how to go about this. One gifted aerospace engineer spent most of his leisure enmeshed in exceptionally useful ideas, but none of them came to fruition. Ten years before we knew of "hang gliders" he was adapting a "Rogallo wing" to sport use, trying out little kites with various weights and strings behind an old VW convertible. He was gifted at research and at melding other ideas and research in new, more useful forms. But he was not adept with his hands. At work this didn't matter because others were; in his own home-based projects, though, it was the difference between success and failure. The models were never built quite properly, so they never flew. When he designed a boat made of cardboard honeycomb and fiberglass, he ran afoul of compound curves, so he kicked the offending material into a corner of the garage with the shards of the hang glider. Today he writes that he is combining windmills and little saillike parachutes floating downwind to create cheap, wind-driven electrical generators—but he knows they won't get built. If a gifted ideas man like this could team himself up with a good chairman and a good implementer (preferably one skilled at electrical and mechanical work), more of us would have access to useful ideas, and the ideas man might have a more interesting life.

One trouble is that the real ideas men are not always the same people who are gifted at group work, or at selling their ideas to other people so subtly they slide under the NIH (Not Invented Here) threshold. People who are adept at implementing other people's ideas are also likely to be the sorts who want some of the credit for themselves.

One way around this conundrum is to find ways for an entire group to get credit for an innovation and to build into the informal reward system (the recognition side of it) considerable recognition for the ongoing achievement as well as the initial idea.

In the case of the scout troop, it started up with not just one driving force but a well-chosen committee of capable, efficient people. The committee met for lunch or dinner and enjoyed one another's company while a lot of informal information flowed about their mutual problems getting the troop going. Though they apportioned out the work, each one understood from the beginning how his own tasks fit into the overall picture, and thus the necessity to develop a substitute/successor as quickly as possible. Close contact with the young members of the troop kept their enthusiasm and sense of responsibility high. In this case, the ideas man was able to act as a low-key chairman, to build a self-sustaining organization.

Moonlight Projects and Bootleg Babies

Many of the most interesting innovations I've run across (including the Rogallo wing, the cardboard boat, and the sail-driven windmill) are bootlegged. The engineer was actually managing a large project in the aerospace industry but felt too far removed from designing things; now and then creative instinct would creep to the surface, and he would scribble on the backs of envelopes and read old copies of *Scientific American* and then disappear into his playmate-lined garage workshop. Until the energy crisis, his company was unlikely to have much interest in these little projects, which were more like avocations. But if it *had* taken an interest, or permitted certain resources and team members to be filched for such notions, it might be more successfully diversified today.

Many products emerge inside companies in just this way. Someone has an idea. He knows as soon as his delicate idea gets into the formal system it is going to be subjected to scrutiny, analysis, and all kinds of unkind stresses and strains. So he keeps it under his bench or in his bottom drawer and sneaks time away from formal assignments to refine it a little or test it some more. I've seen people write brilliant little computer programs to snitch a bit of calculation for highly technical aspects of bootleg babies.

A gifted manager—and sometimes a gifted organization—finds ways to look the other way when bootleg babies are still too young and tender to be exposed to the formalities of a firm's product development machinery. The tender young thing needs care and feeding. "A face that only a mother could love," you might say. So the gifted manager, if his innovator is capable of carrying on without help for a while, simply says: "Don't tell me too much at this stage; I don't want to know. Just make sure X and Y aren't neglected while you're working on this one as well. And for all our sakes, make sure nobody over in the other department hears about it!"

Eventually, the bootleg baby gets pink-cheeked and its nurturer is proud of the healthy thing. That's when the gifted manager might want to take a private look. If he admires the baby, he's already rewarding the innovator; more important, if a little more in the way of development resources might make a difference, this is the stage for informal bootlegging on a higher order. "OK, you can have John and Dick to help a little, but make sure it doesn't appear on their time cards. I think we could borrow some test instruments from Al's group; I'll speak to him after work tonight."

Step by step, the innovation comes out from under the bench into the daylight, as a little group makes the baby its own, then a larger group begins to take interest, and eventually avuncular pride in this development of their own. Selling the ownership is the first stage in testing, proving, and improving it for the next element up in the hierarchy or (often more pertinent) across it.

Bootleg babies and moonlight projects often have much more drive behind them than planned products simply because nobody has to "motivate" the innovator who has done it all for his own psychological reasons, and because the challenge of doing something slightly forbidden or frowned upon adds its own zest to the process, and because the moonlight/bootleg approach permits the baby to grow organically, rather than according to some predetermined plan. On the other hand, once such a product reaches the surface, the formal processes in the organization, it is often much harder to adapt or change to fit new needs or markets than a committee-designed, formally specified innovation. The "owner" usually resists any implication that his original design is less than perfect, just like a mother refusing to notice that her baby is slightly, charmingly cross-eyed.

Four Generations of Managers

Bootlegging is particularly rampant—and necessary—in large organizations. In the small firm, based on the bootleg baby (often designed while the innovator worked for some other firm that didn't or wouldn't appreciate it), the "others" from whom the baby must be protected are outside the walls, and the entire little company might be considered a "nursery" for a baby whose worth may eventually be proved in the marketplace.

I watched one such firm grow from a handful of scrappy technical people to a few thousand employees. In retrospect, I think it took different types of people to manage at different stages of growth. As with the group members in Chapter 14, some characteristics of each generation are innate, but most people can operate in two phases (seldom more, effectively). Most people would recognize for themselves their natural "generation"—and many of the management casualties I've seen are probably people who were taken over or merged into a stage of corporate growth beyond their natural habitat.

The First-Generation Manager is likely to double as loyal company secretary, dishwasher, cheerleader, and deliveryman. (I'm leaving aside the founder, who is already envisioning how to spend his not-yet-made millions.) He came in with the founder or shortly thereafter because he was fed up in the constricting environment of a larger company. Often, because he's a pioneer, he gets stock options that add to his emotional ties and keep him glued to the company no matter what. His strengths are versatility, flexibility, and probably lots of ambition; he may also be a trifle naive, a refugee from the corporate environment that demands political skills.

The Second-Generation Manager is probably a hungry young tiger, delighted to find a little company that will give him room to swing. He's flexible and versatile, too, but more important, he has a vision of taking the little company into the big time. He'll work night and day to get orders out the door as the growth continues and more people squeeze into the rented quarters. He, too, may have some stock options, but they won't be as big as the pioneers had, which he may resent as they disappear into small back offices and his production or marketing skills drive the revenues up the graphs. He's not always as adept at coordination but makes up for it in enthusiasm and drive.

The Third-Generation Manager has to come in to bring order out of the chaos that the First and Second wrought as the company grew. He brings a more analytical skill, some accounting, and some systems savvy. He's likely, as was the Second-Generation man, to be an alumnus of a larger company, but his reasons for moving—later—are somewhat more orderly. He likes being needed but minds when he feels the order he's bringing is not appreciated—as it seldom is when a company goes through the transition from Second to Third Generation. He may be *too* systematic and insensitive to the culture of the company or its folklore. With his arrival, in-house politics increases.

The Fourth-Generation Manager, smooth as the silk shirts he might wear, comes in only if the company has become so successful it has been absorbed into some giant firm. His skills are human and political, translating to people in the company the expectations of their new partners or masters, and helping keep an umbrella over those portions of the company that are not yet ready for scrutiny from large-company experts. He may have to be a hatchet man as well as impose systems that are different from those the company evolved for itself during the pains of the Third Generation.

I think each of these caricatures is a necessary addition at some stage as a company grows. One of the small tragedies of the heady days of high technology in the sixties was the number of First- and Second-Generation managers who were locked into Third-Generation companies by their stock options, which didn't vest for a number of years. The purpose of the option was originally to motivate him and to give him a reason for staying with the risky little operation. But the better the company succeeds, the less it appreciates the skills and loyalty of a pioneer; it might be much more humane as well as helpful to growing, changing organizations to have a "mutual choice" clause that allows the man to depart gracefully, with all his shares, before his years of incarceration are up—a kind of parole clause.

Similarly, it might be fruitful in the early days of a company to set aside a few stock options similar in size to those being bestowed on First- or Second-Generation managers for those who will inevitably come later. The imbalances in a company that is succeeding can create situations even more difficult than the natural differences between different-generation managers.

One other aspect of the generation game may be worth exploring. Because companies in different stages behave so differently, it might be helpful to consider developing people by sending them across these *generation boundaries*. Several large firms are today helping small companies in their communities by finding managers who are willing to be advisors, part time or full time. Such managers almost always say they are learning more than they are teaching. Shell International actually has a three-week course for its own people in which they act as consultants to small firms. The learning is high, and the number of small companies queueing to be seen by the big-company people is increasing.

Too Much Stability?

We've discussed the growth of an idea and selling it to a group so it can become self-sustaining and the growth of a company through its various generations. The latter process might actually work better if people at each generation brought their innovations in with the same care the boot-legger has to lavish on his group—making sure that the ownership was widely shared before anything formal was announced.

What happens, though, if a self-sustaining group or organization is *too* good at maintaining itself? In genetics, DNA exists to replicate exactly the same pattern in the next generation; a self-sustaining company has built systems and procedures and a culture that efficiently reproduce the necessary patterns to ensure continuing success. The leaders hire *doppelgangers* or "ghostly doubles" who even wear similar costumes. But times change; the ice ages come and go, and one of DNA's most lovable properties is its occasional mutations, the little flaws and accidents of nature that make the off-spring ever so slightly *different* from the parent, in spite of the elegant templates. Some of those mutations can help an offspring survive when the outside conditions have changed —the furrier mastodon babies were better suited to ice ages.

When an organization is too perfect at replicating itself, too vigilant in stamping out mutations, it may actually endanger its survival—as many companies learned in the last recession.

Leadership is certainly the key to self-sustaining organizations. An ancient Chinese saying, attributed to Lao-tzu around 600 B.C., sums up this ageless question:

> A leader is best when he is neither seen nor heard. Not so good when he is adored or glorified. Worst when he is hated or despised. Fail to honor your people and they will fail to honor you. But of a good leader when his work is done, his aim fulfilled, the people will all say: "We did this ourselves."

Chapter 18.

STABILITY AND CHANGE

To meet the eighties, organizations will have to change. This means opening up, flattening down, loosening up, and at the same time tightening down, producing more things with fewer people, increasing productivity without increasing uproar. A delicate balancing act at best, and one that will be most difficult in some of the larger companies that have learned to think big.

When people are worried or afraid, they freeze. They resist change of any kind. They cling to tradition, security, any symbol that the world is not passing them by, that it has not become unmanageable. Thus, in difficult times (and most companies will have some difficult times in the next few years), even though change becomes more imperative, it becomes less possible.

When people are having fun, when they feel they are winning, they open up, welcome new ideas, and look for ways to create new symbols. Thus, the organization that is already yeasty has even more opportunity to change, and the problem becomes one of keeping order.

It's a kind of yin/yang situation, balancing an organization between the tendency to freeze, looking inward, and the tendency to fly apart with all the centrifugal energy—avoiding vicious circles in either direction.

John Morris at the Manchester Business School has a little model that helps me think about organizations in these terms.

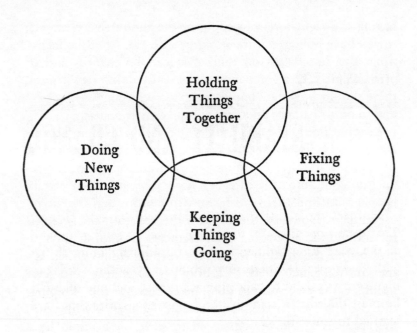

Holding
Things
Together

Doing
New
Things

Fixing
Things

Keeping
Things
Going

These activities interweave but they are really different kinds of activities and they require different kinds of people. Each is important in its way, and at different times different activities seem more crucial, but the real picture includes some of all of them most of the time.

Holding things together is the general management task, making sure that information from one element flows freely into all the other elements it impinges upon, keeping an eye on the boundaries between different elements, making sure they speak the same language. The elements might be entitled "lab," "production," and "customer service" or any other set of titles, but the general manager has to see them in relation to each other, as well as managing each one as an entity.

Doing new things is the innovation we've already discussed. Some kinds of people and groups thrive on it naturally; others have to be brought to it much more gently because it's not their innate environment. Half the battle is having the right sorts of people in the innovative elements, so you have human nature working with you from the beginning. But innovators on their own can be chaotic, and in every element of a company that is really doing new things, there should be some "implementers" and some "inspectors" and so on to balance and channel the creative energy.

Keeping things going is usually the backbone of an organization, the various departments that are taken for granted at best, unless they get in trouble. Some functions (such as production) fall into this category naturally and often attract people who find their satisfaction in continuing, repetitive, useful tasks. However, the trick for the general managers and for individuals managing such elements is finding ways to give people recognition for simply keeping things going. It's the kind of game where "winning" is not likely, and "not losing" is the best you can do. The epitome of the "keeping-things-going" job might be a place on the assembly line, and the epitome of the person suited to such a job might be a well-trained mentally retarded person who found great satisfaction in making the same motions efficiently all day. However, very few production lines are manned by handicapped people, so there is a real challenge for management in making the work satisfying to alert, often innovative types whose opportunities to have fun are usually channeled into making things stop working so well.

Fixing things or "trouble-shooting" is what happens if the people who have been keeping things going don't do so. "Things" in this case could be as esoteric as a department with employee relations problems or as mundane as a broken machine. Whether the tools are organizational, mechanical, chemical, or electronic, though, the types of people who enjoy fixing things are unique. If their special talents aren't recognized, I have known some who are perfectly capable of helping things get out of kilter so they can have something to fix.

Actually, this "maintenance" task, undersung as in the production task, requires certain steps, whether you're maintaining a person or a car or a department. First, the maintenance man gathers together all the information about the problem and immerses himself in whatever kinds of diagrams or lists there are to describe the way the thing ought to work. Then he gathers together all the tools and materials that are going to be needed for the job. Then he does the job. Then he mops up afterwards. This sounds very simple, but it's a process I learned from watching a fine mechanic working on an MGB for a number of weekends, and the revelation was how many other jobs I had short-shrifted by ignoring the fact-finding, tools-and-materials, or mopping-up phases. "Doing it" looks easy, but it isn't if you don't have the right-size monkey wrench or some clean rags handy or the nasty green stuff to get the grease off your hands and bumpers afterwards. The same principles seem to hold true whether I'm sewing a dress, writing a chapter, or fixing the broken window sash cord—and they hold true even more when the thing that needs fixing is a malfunctioning group or organization.

These treasured people who fix things up in organizational terms seem to have a sixth sense, like my mechanic friend's finely tuned ear, that notes little knocks and grumbles before they are obvious to others. They don't depend as much on instruments (or attitude surveys or appraisal systems) as they do on this instinct. I remember one factory in Amsterdam which had passed all its attitude surveys with flying colors, but the training manager felt there was some dissatisfaction lurking beneath the surface. He trained several other managers to listen carefully and started a series of interviews with people on the shop-floor. In the long run, after a careful period of diagnosis and discussion, the employees took part in a grand redesign of the factory into smaller, more autonomous working groups. Productivity went up sharply, and so did the pleasant hum of the factory.

Although there was a perfectly good canteen, the workers began to raid the office wing for tables and chairs, pleasantly mismatched, on which to sip their coffee and talk over the day's production or its problems. Management eventually offered to buy them matched furniture for their self-designed coffee areas, but the employees disdained the matched sets, preferring their pilfered "perks" (the British slang for "management perquisites" up to and including the chauffeured Rolls-Royce). When I visited the factory it was impressive for the assortment of posters (from pigs to pin-ups) in the different working areas, as well as houseplants and the occasional goldfish. I had just come from a superbly orderly factory in Germany, with row on row of desks or benches, never an inch out of line, and not one single postcard on the walls or messy desk to denote individuality. It was nice to find out that the productivity had risen in the Amsterdam factory by astonishing amounts, partly as a result of doing away with all the systems to measure productivity.

Changes seem to come in cycles. Berg suggests that periods of revolution are natural in an organization, preceded and followed by periods of stability. As is mid-life crisis, the potential for rapid change is probably lurking inside most organizations, simply waiting to be triggered after they reach a certain point. Sometimes the change is healthy, and sometimes it seems disastrous; sometimes it's planned, and sometimes it's something that wells up out of the organization of its own accord.

Some of the most important imperatives for change are more likely to be structural than cyclic. The improved health and education of the work force everywhere in the industrialized world has brought about a permanent change in people's expectations, and they will not revert to old values and old ways. They want to work less and be paid more. (This may be fortuitous, if the shift from work ethic to leisure ethic can be accomplished gradually enough. Rapid advances in "productivity" are likely to make unemployment problems worse in the near term, no matter what the economic situation.) They want a larger say in their own working lives as well as their leisure lives. They want less bureaucratic control from the government, the community, and the employer. Like the camel sticking just his nose under the tent, organizations will find that just a little flexitime or just a little disclosure of financial results or just a little employee consultation will infiltrate and cause uproar if the tent isn't prepared to accommodate that particular camel and his humpy implications.

Whether the problem is slowing it down or speeding it up, the key word in coping with these changes is "gradual." Pascale writes:

> The notion of achieving gradual change, rather than launching a head-on assault, runs deep in Eastern culture. It provides a manager with a context of thinking about outflanking organizational obstacles and in time letting them wither away. "It is well to persist like water," counsels the Tao saying. "For back it comes, again and again, wearing down the rigid strength which cannot yield to withstand it."

Chapter 19.

CRITICAL MASS

"What is the sound of one hand clapping?" asks the old Zen Buddhist koan. Its modern organizational analogy might be the lone voice of the future, wandering unheard in the long halls, surrounded by people concerned only about the present. Another all-too-familiar analogy is the lone participant in some splendid management course, dashing home with all his new wisdom and/or know-how, to find there's no one interested. Or as the Zen Buddhists put it in another koan: "If a tree falls in the forest and there is no one around to hear, does it make a sound?"

Something funny happens when a social phenomenon reaches "critical mass." Suddenly, everyone is talking about something that was obscure and unknown last week or last month. My son comes back from Boston with a taste for "Harvey Wallbangers," or Miss America is selected with a unique combination of health and religion emphases, and another set of social trends is made explicit.

One step in bringing about change, on almost any scale, is to create a shared body of values, attitudes, or experiences, a new "membership" in which individuals reinforce one another in using, extending, or defending a new idea against the pull of inertia, tradition, reluctance, or outright opposition. To make use of the idea of critical mass, we need to borrow from physics, from advertising, from psychology, and from common sense.

In physics, "critical mass" is the amount of uranium you need to put together to start an atomic reaction. If you get enough of it together fast enough you get a dilly of a bomb.

If you just edge over the threshold, with lots of controls, you may get manageable energy. I suspect it's much easier to build A-bombs than nuclear power stations. As I recall from first semester physics in the olden days, you could get energy from fusion—putting elements together—or from fission—blasting them to smithereens.

In advertising, a whole industry has grown up to grow bandwagons and keep them rolling. Every magazine or television ad is subtly telling me I'm not quite OK if I don't look like this or wear that or use the other to keep my floors sparkling. But I don't respond to all the messages; indeed, some set up a counterresponse. So what is it that determines which Scotch or which brand of jogging shoes or which kind of car is necessary to my self-image? The sense of bandwagon might be enhanced by the ads, but the ads are just reinforcing the informal information, the chat machinery, from which I'm already receiving messages about what's OK and what's very OK and what's not OK at all. The more hooks the ads have, in language and pictures, into my own images about that informal machinery, the more likely I am to respond "positively" (i.e., with anxiety) to the ads.

The psychology books are full of examples of how a group's thinking can influence an individual. The one I recall best has naughty elements: most members of the group are really shills, playing with the house money, pre-programmed to have a particular set of opinions, or to see a particular thing in an ink-blot (or to believe that the emperor is sumptuously clothed). When the subject hears those around him express a view that does not correlate with his own observations, he usually decides his own observations must be faulty, so he goes along with the group, sometimes to quite outrageous lengths. In this case "critical mass" is a relative matter; it can be quite a small number, so long as it amounts to everyone else in the room except me.

This is where the common sense comes in. To change things in a group or organization, you often need to build a critical mass of people who agree with you and each other that the change is vital and positive. One way to get that critical mass quickly and easily is to start with a small, clearly identified group, whose members already look to one another as people of sound, wise views. Once an idea can be planted and sprouted in such a group and grown to some demonstrable maturity, it will have much better chances of being transplanted to other groups.

To plant an idea in a group, you usually start with the most influential member, the "thought leader" to whom other members often look for signposts. (This may or may not be the "ideas man," depending on how many of his ideas are cast aside as not quite yet or not quite right; more often it's the shaper or chairman.) Once he has invented your idea, the group probably has a chance to invent it for themselves. Carrying the model one step further, if the group you've chosen is in turn a "thought leader" within the organization, it is much easier to spread something further, faster.

You start with the most influential member and work quickly out to other key members of a group, and so it is with organizations; if several influential groups almost simultaneously start doing something in a different way, or talking about a new concept, more people in other groups are more likely to hear about it from more of their own informal sources, and the sense of trendiness, of "everybody's doing it," is enhanced. This seems to work not on an additive basis, but on a multiplicative basis. If I hear a key word once this week and once next week I've heard it twice; but if I hear it three times this week from different sources, suddenly it seems to pop up everywhere, simply because my social sensors have created a new storage cell in my brain to process information about this new trend. So, in the most trivial instance, I cautiously try one Harvey Wallbanger and then shift wholeheartedly from old-hat Boodles-with-a-twist to the new tipple; then I, in turn, begin to offer Wallbangers to my friends, and the trend gains a little momentum from my own anxious desire to be "with it," if not trendy.

There are groups and individuals who pride themselves on good old values, on holding out against trends, but even they help reinforce the sense of trend by holding out. Once I have to explain why Glenfiddich is so much better than a Harvey Wallbanger, I'm doing just as much to fuel the Wallbanger trend as if I were going along with it. Similarly, in organizations it is sometimes the most recalcitrant blockers of change who can be the most effective aids to change agents, either by being seen to block a change too stubbornly, or by being seen to be converted.

So the first step to achieving critical mass is to control the population size. This is one more reason to avoid announcementitis, to work through the informal machinery in organization change long before it reaches formal stages. Converting key individuals and clustering them together, then developing separate clusters and linking them, letting the word-of-mouth messages of success seep out long before any formal claims are made—these are some of the steps in the first phase.

Another factor that can help achieve critical mass in an organization is a sense of crisis, or at least concern. It is much easier to bring about major changes in style and culture during hard times than it is when things are going well. "Why change a winning game?" people ask, even though the change might help them win much more in the long run. This may seem slightly strange, because individual reactions during hard times are to retrench, seek for security, turn to tried-and-true ways, and I've already noted that a winning team will be much more eager to try new things. But at the level of the entire organization, or in a troubled industry, it seems to work the other way around. Only when a sense of crisis has itself reached the stage of critical mass, when the problems can no longer be swept under the rugs, are people really willing to talk about the underlying problems in the culture or the style or their relationships with each other—and those are the kinds of organizational changes we're really talking about. Then the reaction seems to be: "Things can't get much worse, and so we might as well try this; they might get better."

A sense of concern or tension has another aspect that can be helpful to a change agent. It is somehow more acceptable to bring in people from the outside, whether they be experts, or simply mirrors from other corporate cultures, when times are clearly difficult. People can accept the outsider's presence without losing face if a large enough population (a "critical mass" on a different scale) shares the sense that there are troubles.

The concept of critical mass is essential to organizational change, but it contains some funny quirks. One major chemical company, for example, has created a series of outside courses for its managers, to create a critical mass of people who share a picture of where the company is headed and what a manager's role will be within it. Hundreds of the managers will eventually go through the innovative curriculum, in groups of about twelve, from different divisions and departments and locations. What the company will end up with will actually be a honey of a network—but virtually no sense of critical mass. They'll see each other back at work wearing the old school tie, and chat about interesting experiences they had on their different sessions of the course and get to know one another better. But they won't feed one another's sense of imperative change. Going to the same place at different times gives a sense of remote connection but not the shared-experience (shared-hangover) brotherhood that you need to take new energy from the connection, to feed a critical mass of action-oriented people.

If such a course were to be used to build a sense of critical mass, I think it would need one simple difference. Instead of twelve people from twelve different corners of the company, each group should consist of two sixes or four threes, starting with pairs or clusters from a single working element of the company. If these clusters were started within a single location or department and worked out in patterns that matched the organization's own interrelationships, it would be possible to use the course to initiate and maintain a sense of imminence, importance, involvement in the changes, and perhaps a pioneering, elite feeling as well.

This aspect of critical mass has much wider implications in management education, I believe. Since a large proportion of people who are sent on middle-manager courses are actually looking for ways to improve their organizations or groups, I believe that they could be sent in pairs or clusters with much better effect than the lonesome individual can create when he comes back from any course, no matter how smooth or rough his re-entry. The returning pairs or trios or quartets can then reinforce each other's sense of crisis, of challenge, of change and the patterns it should take, and because those with whom they work are hearing the message from more than one voice, it takes on added importance within the manageable-size working population.

One large engineering company used action learning to create a cadre of middle managers who could succeed the aging top managers. About fifty people went through the program in the course of several years and wafted out into different parts of the company, carrying some useful concepts about projects and self-development with them, often starting useful little activities in their own departments. But it was not until three of the elite young managers accidentally found themselves in a single location, dealing with major problems, that they actually became a "center of heresy," protecting one another, energizing one another and those around them, and creating a focus for organizational change on a much wider scale.

Chapter 20.

CHANGE AGENTS

"This is our change agent," said the personnel director proudly. A large man stood up, grinning and stretching out his hand enthusiastically, as a shower of papers fell from his knee, the table, and the briefcase he upset standing up. He seemed too visible, too big to be a silent, hidden change agent, the pattern I had in the back of my mind. He was too open to be wily, too nice to be clever.

I watched him operate during the next year or so and learned a bit more about change agentry. I also learned, as did he, that a single individual so denoted in a company that really doesn't want change is like the token lady on the board, the "black by the door," a symbol without substance. The change agent spent several more years in uphill battles and sometimes head-on confrontations, trying to make his company more participative; employees often changed, but managers didn't. He was walled off in smaller and less important bits of the company. Eventually, he went into business for himself, older, wiser, and now considerably wealthier.

Given the variety of boundaries that must be crossed and the behavior and attitudes that must be shifted to cope with the complex future, we are going to need many more people who understand change, both downwards and upwards, and can help it to happen. This raises questions of how to find them and grow them, how they can work from inside and outside organizations, and what kind of support they need to operate effectively.

To explore these questions I convened several workshops including a number of people who had demonstrated an ability to help organizations change, in half a dozen different countries. Most of the material in this chapter comes directly from the change agents themselves, but the description of a change agent is my own, derived from watching them en masse.

Defining a change agent is difficult, and describing what he does is complicated. It might be best to create a composite prototype. He is a discontented optimist, impatient with bureaucracy and traditional constraints. He is also patient enough to live with incremental change rather than revolution. He (more rarely "she") is confident, with a "helping" attitude and high tolerance for ambiguity, impermanence, and risk. He's often egotistical, but gets his boost by low-profile and sometimes wily successes in getting others to take credit for achievements or ownership of changes that are really his own doing. He has experienced major job and culture changes, probably several times. He may spend a lot of energy on unpaid work or good deeds outside his normal job. He often demonstrates a well-developed sense of design or aesthetics. He is curious about new cultures, people, and ideas. He's skilled at translating from one jargon to another and builds word-pictures people can understand across boundaries. He may be benignly manipulative, though a good many simply operate on the basis that: "This is what I do; take it or leave it." He'll cut corners if he believes people will benefit in the long run but he often questions the ethics of what he's doing. An energetic person himself, he seems to understand energy in the organization, and where to tap it.

The change agent likes theories and models. A voluminous body of his management literature about "organization development" or "OD" needs to be de-ODorized before outsiders can understand and use it—and he's unlikely to do the job for them. In practice, he doesn't operate the way his shelves of books and articles would indicate. The stereotypical OD man values "here and now," openness, honesty, "feedback," "confronting," and so on. In reality, the change agent is likely to be a good politician, bouncing among roles as necessary. Instead of having a massive vision of the overall scheme, he tends to fly by the seat of his pants, seldom planning more than a week ahead. He goes much more by intuition than his literature would have it. He doesn't always confront issues and he often works in the "there and then" instead of the "here and now." Instead of acting as a mirror for members of the organization, to help them develop their own pictures of their world, he often tries to transmit his own picture if he can. In truth, he's really more intuitive and instinctive—more yin, more right-hemisphere—than he would like to believe.

When he is described this way he begins to sound more like a lively manager and less like a mysterious wizard. Some of the most effective change agents are, in fact, line managers trying to shift their own units, or the larger organization as well, into more fruitful directions. Incidentally, among the professional change agents I was able to convene, there was distinct discomfort at the name itself:

> Most managers will run a mile if you call yourself "change agent" or "consultant." They only run half a mile from "trainer" or "management developer." Those titles just aren't perceived as central to the real power and issues.

> I like "change assistant" or "learning assistant." That reverses the doctor/patient image and makes it clear you're just helping in someone else's change.

> The "change agent" or "OD man" may be viewed as a manipulator, and the term "agent" implies someone else's man. I prefer "catalyst," which has a sound basis in chemical interactions.

They're all demonstrating the change agent's sensitivity to

words and images, and awareness that the idea of change itself threatens people.

Prophets Without Profit

Defining a change agent is inextricably entwined with what he does. One personnel director says:

> Managers are like seeds. If you keep them in the packet they'll never germinate. You recruit them and develop them and plant them out in the company and some of them take root. The question is to find out how we can make more of our seeds germinate. Call it OD, change agentry, whatever you like, but it's nothing new. It's just a way of focusing attention on how to grow your organization. If we succeed we'll be able to help more people value the changes—and that means we'll be changing the value system.

One expert says a change agent is one who goes around building missing institutions, looking for the thing that's not there (such as a new definition for "industrial relations") and then designing it. Another calls them "entrepreneurs without a business." Another points out that they seldom have profit-centered visibility, so they are "prophets without profit in their own companies." On the other hand, the "agent of change" may be a factor in the outside environment —a hurricane or a new regulation—that demands response, and the catalyst simply helps speed the response, like the enzyme in the human cell.

In one basic respect the change agent has a different viewpoint from the chairman or chief executive or legislator who talks about change on the premise that he knows what is best for "the people." The typical change agent may work this way occasionally, but he espouses the belief that "the people" know what is best for themselves, given some chance to think about it, and he is in much more frequent contact with "the people."

Certain personality characteristics seem essential for the effective change agent:

* He is *aware*, sensitive to the need for change, what its effects might be across boundaries, where the blockages are likely to be, and how they might be turned into helpful energy.

* He is *entrepreneurial*. In French the word "entrepreneur" means "one who stages dramas." In Swedish it is "one who builds a building." In English it implies high creativity, seizing opportunities. In organization terms he is probably a "social entrepreneur," managing a change but also acting as merchant, trader, broker—and taking a percentage in one way or another.

* His payoff comes in *recognition or self-development* more often than money. But he is willing to share his own recognition with others, or give it up entirely if that gives him more power (or opportunity) to bring about change.

* He is *empathetic*, accepting or even cherishing people for their foibles. All the change agents I convened had plenty of foibles of their own and tended to like themselves anyway. He is likely to admit his failings openly and thus alleviate other people's guilts and anxieties about their own.

* He is a *link-man* between different departments or inside/outside or among functions or between top and bottom levels. He prefers the richness of an analogy like "connective tissue" or "nervous system" rather than emphasis on single links.

* He is a *mature outsider*, even within his own organization. One says: "I want to behave so I don't get labeled 'a nut' but to be different enough to be help-

ful." Another says: "It's easier to get a revolution going in a pin-striped suit." A third adds: "Revolution means changing the value system; rebellion might be pushing for more space within it. Evolution takes patience."

Mature themselves, change agents view other people as mature and positive, given the opportunity. Thus, they tend to think in terms of participation. Almost every one can give some example of employees who opted for development opportunities rather than money, or were motivated by chances to improve the general good rather than their own.

Basic Skills for Change Agentry

How do they do whatever they do, and how much of their instinctive or informal know-how can be passed on to others? We found three different change roles: (a) the butterfly or link-man, who works from outside, facilitating connections among different institutions; (b) the boundary manager, sensing across his own boundaries and painting pictures or scenarios for people on both sides; and (c) the inside catalyst or "prophet without honor," helping changes within his own organization or one element of it. That may be the most difficult role of all because the outside expert who comes in at the behest of top management has less risk and can assume (not always correctly) that his client shares his values, but the insider takes more risk and seldom feels that top management is really behind him.

A few quotes from participants in my workshops indicate their emphasis and how they exercise it:

> "Try to involve other people in the problem, so it becomes their idea."

> "Remember to pose the problem, not the solution."

> "Start from where the other guy is."

"To do any real good I had to influence the culture of the company."

"Try to get every senior manager and division chief involved."

"I go and look in the wrong places. That's where you get your surprises."

In one instance the change agent helped start "vertical slice" courses for everyone in the factory from the toilet cleaner to the production manager. "That helped get rid of the chips on people's shoulders." By involving 150 people his team was able to design a totally new organization for the factory.

Although he doesn't always spend much time introspecting about his own role, the change agent is usually skilled at getting other people to think about their roles and their interactions in a group. He usually has a "bag of tricks" to help him. (Some of these are discussed in the next chapter.)

His bag of tricks also includes techniques to help groups create a climate in which ideas generate and convert themselves into action. Some of these might be such things as brainstorming, "synectics" (another word for using analogies), attribute listing, or check lists. At the same time he has to exercise and pass on the art of building support and create a sense of excitement without overinflating people's expectations.

The change agent's most useful attribute may be his ability to build a network of networks, making change agents of others. In one example the engineering and maintenance people from a number of unions in a large, multi-plant site had suffered jurisdictional disputes, squabbles, and strikes for some years. Tony Treadgold, an experienced line manager who understood the company and the situation, asked to go in as personnel manager. It took him five years, building gradually, to help the organization shift toward a cooperative stance, in which there were no more inter-union strikes and people were enthusiastically involved in develop-

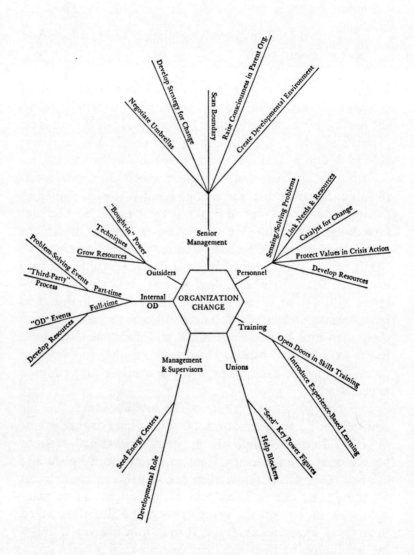

ORGANIZATION CHANGE

Senior Management
- Negotiate Umbrellas
- Develop Strategy for Change
- Scan Boundary
- Raise Consciousness in Parent Org.
- Create Developmental Environment

Personnel
- Sensing/Solving Problems
- Link Needs & Resources
- Catalyst for Change
- Protect Values in Crisis Action
- Develop Resources

Training
- Open Doors in Skills Training
- Introduce Experience-Based Learning

Unions
- "Seed" Key Power Figures
- Help Blockers

Management & Supervisors
- Developmental Role
- Seed Energy Centers

Internal OD
- Full-time
  - "OD" Events
  - Develop Resources
- Part-time
  - Problem-Solving Events
  - "Third-Party" Process

Outsiders
- Grow Resources
- Techniques
- "Bought-in" Power

194 /

ing themselves as well as their team. Tony drew the preceding map to describe all the people inside and out who eventually became active catalysts in the five-year process.

Potential change agents exist all over the organization's landscape. Growing them is an organic process—more akin to the compost heap than to the laboratory fertilizer. In this case Treadgold mentioned the importance of starting with a conceptual framework that fits the organization; his was "open systems planning." In other companies it might be "systems thinking" or "developing helicopter quality" or "managerial grid" or some other generally approved language. Then he began using a variety of techniques to grow more involvement:

* getting off the site in groups,

* using people part time (they maintain credibility and puncture boundaries),

* using outside consultants to confer credibility on the insiders,

* using inside people as consultants (to develop them as well as solve problems and increase their individual credibility),

* spotting the "blockers" and listening to them (which often neutralizes their opposition and turns some into powerful helpers),

* building and protecting "centers of heresy," and

* exposing the values of one group to another (they understand each other better and often turn out to be similar).

From Treadgold's case and others we were able to derive a picture of the basic skills and aptitudes a potential change agent should have. None of these, incidentally, are skills one can develop in formal courses.

One is the *ability to raise people's consciousness.* "There may be a link between consciousness-raising and discontent with the status quo. You want to share your better perception by sharing your discontent," said one.

Another necessity is the *ability to use language and symbols*—and note the confluence of *both* halves of the brain here—to make people see the situation in a totally new way. One example might be Ralph Nader with the simple but memorable title *Unsafe at Any Speed.* This is closely related to the *ability to amplify.* "With a tiny symbol of change you can get a huge change in people's confidence," the change agents agreed. In one case the plant manager gave complaining workers about $100 to "do something" about poor working conditions. They spent the weekend painting their part of the plant, and further changes spread out from there.

Another basic skill is the *ability to see an emerging process* early, and make others aware of it—a skill that someone called "social empathy."

The *ability to change people's view of themselves,* from powerless ciphers into people who might be timid but are nonetheless willing to talk to top management and transcend organization boundaries, is vital. I used to call this "holding up a mirror," but as we shall discuss in the next chapter, it is more often an act of painting a picture, or at least drawing a cartoon that people recognize as themselves (whether *you* think it's a good likeness is less important, if you're the change agent). One participant called this "role consultation."

A crucial skill is the *ability to operate at different levels in the organization.* "If you're not looking into at least three levels, you can't achieve much," was Derek Sheane's comment. This requires the *ability to learn the language* at each level, and to put on the disguises used at that level. Underlying this discussion was the need for the change agent to keep his direct line open to sources of power. Most had learned this by uncomfortable experience.

A *sense of timing* is imperative, simply part of a basic sensitivity. This means sensing how fast or how slow change must be to be properly rooted, yet maintain credibility.

And *credibility*—upwards, downwards, and sideways—was the most pressing concern of every change agent at the workshop. Building it and maintaining it, both personally and for a specific activity, is central to their work. Credibility, they say, is a combination of personal attributes, skill in building a reputation, and opportunities for experience and language-building.

Finally, they identified the *ability to construct coalitions*. (They felt academics are seldom experienced at constructing pragmatic coalitions. Academic values tend more to individual achievements than group achievements.) One cited Reg Revans' "coalition of power" for crossing boundaries:

* The power of knowledge (you have to find out who knows about the problem)

* The power of emotion (who cares about it?)

* The power of organization (who can *do* something about it?)

Insider/outsider coalitions are particularly important. One had found a powerful outside consultant who was seen to initiate many new activities. The insider spent a lot of time making the outsider aware of the central currents and culture. "I needed his knowledge of how to change things, and he needed my knowledge of how the organization worked." Another change agent, subject to "management by snowflakes" (of memos, every time his superiors went to outside meetings or conferences), began to cultivate outside executives and plant issues and trends that would filter back to raise consciousness upstairs, rather than try to seed them directly; it worked.

Where Do Change Agents Come From?

If we are to increase our supply of change agents, we need to know what kinds of people they tend to be, and what kinds of backgrounds tend to produce them. Frustration in some form played some part in the early experience of almost every person at the workshops:

> "I felt rebellious because there was so little real work to do."
>
> "I grew upset with the government bureaucracy."
>
> "I was annoyed at the big university, with its big lectures and its heavy machinery."
>
> "I was frustrated in my first job. I felt like a pencil that only wrote what other people were saying."
>
> "I found large organizations constraining me, with 80 percent of the time taken up with 20 percent of the substance. This way I didn't have enough time available to help make things work better."

Often, when companies are interviewing young applicants for jobs, they reject people with such attitudes: "He might be a potential troublemaker." Instead, these people merit a closer look. Something gave them a sense that they owned their own careers. They reacted by going somewhere that looked better, or developing whatever skills it took to improve the bad situation—or usually both. They might be characterized as rebels who matured and accepted evolution. Certainly, they are able to cope with limited, incremental change, with modernization or renovation. And they don't get discouraged easily.

Most of them had an early opportunity to change things —student union, a local government stint, improving a chemical plant at the age of twenty-one, or undertaking a work-study job with teeth. "I got self-confidence and recognition," was the usual comment regarding the early chance for "hairy-chested leadership." Each had experienced (and usually initiated) at least one drastic job change, from one country to another, technical to personnel, large company to self-employment, and so on. Any organization that wants to nurture more change agents might look for more opportunities along these lines for the youngest entrants.

Caring kinds of vocations and avocations were common. Derek Sheane had taught maladjusted adolescents in Northern Ireland. Gerry Van Weelden works with retarded children. Bob Garratt spends at least a quarter of his time in unpaid development work in rural areas in Britain and France. Tony Treadgold is helping a bishop change the organization of a diocese. Richard Cochrane works with disabled people. Peter Frankel counsels university students.

A demystification experience seemed common and may have contributed to later boundary-crossing interest. Ian Cunningham, from a working class background, got involved in student politics nationally. "I met important people and found they were rather ordinary." Ron Halford recalled a working class summer: "I found I could pick as much fruit as an adult." When Peter Frankel was an aspiring young manager sent to Germany to impose the will of Swedish headquarters, he discovered headquarters was wrong and sided with the locals. Ron, a sequestered young technical man in his first management assignment, had to close down a plant: "I found how much you could achieve with what the company believed to be the most useless people." For Gerry, as a middle-class, intellectual young manager, his first assignment with visible responsibility was a surprise: "Everyone in the organization had a lot to contribute; they just hadn't been asked before." Whether the discovery was the clay feet of those on high or the good sense of those below (or both), every change agent had arrived at an egalitarian outlook, as well as the languages of the other half.

Courses *can* help develop change agents once suitable candidates have been found. At ICI about sixty union representatives—already selected through natural processes by their members—have become much more active agents of change after going through a course in "consultancy skills." Various other firms have in-house courses pointed toward making managers into change agents.

The purpose of most of the courses seems to be "licensing" the members, putting on them the seal of corporate approval to go out and indulge in subversive, change-oriented activities, while at the same time sharpening a few skills or adding a few techniques.

Chapter 21.

DO-IT-YOURSELF CONSULTING

One of the best ways I know for an organization to have fun, save money, solve problems, and develop its people is to indulge in a little do-it-yourself consulting. The merits of outsiders have already been mentioned, but every insider can be an outsider to some other part of the company, even if the company is only one hundred people or so.

As I studied change agents I began to find out that many of their techniques would be equally useful in less expert hands, and many of us who do not regard ourselves as "change agents" could nonetheless be useful "consultants" in one way or another. The "expert" model consultant has an obvious kind of know-how to apply to a problem, and you usually bring him in when diagnosis is sufficiently advanced that you know it's his kind of know-how you need. Inside every company there lurk lots of people with specific know-how that might be useful more widely if a model could be found for moving them around now and then without transferring them.

More intriguing, for most companies, is the "innocent" model of the consultant—the one who is selling not his specific know-how but his outsider view, his objectivity and good sense, his ability to see your forest when you're enmeshed in its trees. Sometimes, the less he knows about your own specific culture, technology, and function, the more useful his simple questions may be, because they can reflect back assumptions you might have been taking for granted.

Who *are* the potential do-it-yourself consultants? There are certain functions where a consulting approach is natural:

operations research, systems analysis, and so on. I wish I could add "personnel," but this is too seldom the case. And there are certain personal characteristics that fit people particularly well for this role. One experienced consultant listed the characteristics necessary for his trade as: "a considerable amount of patience, an ability to suffer fools gladly, a flair for finding alternative ways, a talent for anticipating the client's lines of defense, an element of the teacher, and a considerable capacity for logic. Research shows the most effective "helpers" are likely to be a little more disorganized than others, more outgoing, and have a much sharper sense of humor than average. It would be nice to use these guideposts to develop the best possible consultants inside a company; on the other hand, it may be that do-it-yourself consulting can enhance these characteristics in a large population of managers. It's a case of which comes first, the chicken or the egg.

One big bus company, for example, was installing some sparkling new computer systems. One of the directors decided that it might be useful if the "systems analysts" who were the bridge between the computer hardware experts and the user departments (bus scheduling, personnel, vehicle maintenance, and so on) were subservient to the users —not always the approach computer people prefer. So each project was headed up by its user; and every one of the systems analysts was scheduled for a do-it-yourself consulting course that had nothing to do with computing. "Systems analysts should be change agents in the organizational sense, just as much as in the systems sense," said the director.

For these people, experienced already in many parts of the organization and in other organizations before it, the course offered a chance to broaden their thinking, to loosen the constrictions of computer-tied careers. But the course could only be a first step. The development of systems analysts into in-house consultants, or change agents, as does the development of managers, depends most of all on a combination of experience and an occasional mentor. One benefit of courses may simply be to give people time and distance away from everyday demands, to think about the problems that really matter.

A few other techniques are probably worth covering in courses, though experience in an "apprentice" model will make them mean more:

* *Negotiating for space.* Before he does anything else the change agent has to infiltrate the power system for support—before it's needed.

* *Using models, pictures, games.* A good map or model gives the individual the feeling he can have an impact; most OD tools are rather simple, sometimes fun, and they help people look at problems together through the same spectacles.

* *Building coalitions.* How to connect people with shared values, especially between outsiders and insiders.

* *Selling and presentation skills.* These are essential. So is how to run a meeting.

* *Transaction analysis or Gestalt therapy techniques.* Despite the names, these can be useful, and TA (parent/child/adult or "I'm OK, You're OK") is relatively jargon-free.

* *Open Systems Planning.* This is a technical name for a way to help people look in the same mirror. Tony Treadgold uses a dejargonized version of OSP with families, with students, and with church groups. (Perhaps we have to *jargonize* common sense to make such events acceptable to managers?)

Three R's

Once they have some familiarity with a few tools, potential change agents need opportunities to learn by doing.

This means finding more chances for *risk, recognition,* and *responsibility* than the system would normally allow them. Members of task forces or project teams can help. Exposure to other change agents or consultants is important. So is exposure to higher and lower levels in the organization, as often and as intensely as possible.

A mentor with the power to back changes speeds the development, to cushion early failures as well as encourage a little risk. Fear of failure is worse than failure itself. It is certainly a bigger block to someone's development than absence of the opportunity to try. On the other hand, young managers don't learn as much from their failures as they do from their successes, many would contend. And there are risks for the organization if cadres of young tigers are let loose, willy-nilly, to fiddle about with OD and other esoteric interventions into the delicate interrelationships between people and groups. So it's understandable that my "fun and profit" argument would fall on deaf ears in many organizations.

If the training of potential in-house consultants is properly handled, though, and their experience is shared and considered along with some experienced change agents sufficiently often, then I think risk can be minimized for the organization and increased a little for the developing individual. The opportunity to succeed is so vital, and the need for more change agents is increasing so rapidly, that mentors will have to learn to avoid overprotecting the organization. Certain techniques such as T-groups or others that can be threatening to individuals are not suitable for beginning change agents (and many experienced in the role prefer not to use them). But most techniques that simply help people look critically at their own jobs, tasks, and groups and offer them chances for development are much more likely to increase the zest quotient than to endanger relationships.

One experienced change agent summarized the various phases in the development of a confident consultant:

* In the *student* phase he gets interested in Herzberg or McGregor or Berne or some other guru, studies the guru's works, and gradually expands his scope.

* In the *missionary* phase, instead of just listening at the metaphorical feet of the master, he begins to disseminate the wisdom, sometimes slavishly.

* In the *technical* phase other people get fed up hearing about his religion, so he has to become a technician, using some of its mechanisms and devices.

* In the *responsible* phase, if he reaches the point of really responding to other people's needs rather than just doling out his own solutions, he might be called response-able.

* In the *practitioner* phase he has been able to go beyond the technical competence to the stage where he knows and uses the appropriate tools for each problem and is able to improvise as needed.

Many managers could be consultants if the day-to-day demands of organizations didn't limit their freedom of movement. One personnel director has been pushing management development for years and takes pride in his ability to deal with people, but he's risen so high so fast that it's more than ten years since he went on any outside courses or activities himself, ₂nd he's now too important at the center of the company to be spared for any of the consulting-type activities farther out in its line organizations. Simply for the fun of it, he needs a stint of "real work" away from his big office, just the way he needs a holiday every few months. Simply to free up the imagination and creativity of good men, many companies could profit from a do-it-yourself consulting program. The fact that such approaches could make the managers' jobs more satisfying and the fact that the organization itself might become more dynamic and perceptive are added bonuses. Being involved in change is almost always a development opportunity—and at almost every level of an organization, a development opportunity is a strong motivator.

The Art of Listening

The first step in developing consultancy skills is simply to relearn something that is often trained out of managers—the art of listening. This means not only listening to the words (the messages) but also to the fears and feelings behind them (the meta-messages). It can't exactly be taught in courses, and some people are naturally more adept at it than others. On the other hand, any course in consulting skills can give people a chance to practice listening, and thereby to value it more highly. The training of managers in the last several decades has placed much higher value on giving instructions and controlling activities and listening to formal "information," often at the cost of hearing the messages from the other hemisphere of an individual, a group, or even an organization.

You can't say to yourself, or to a group of experienced managers: "You are a lousy listener." So one way to slip this particular stiletto between ribs (yours or theirs) is to call listening "interviewing skills." Brian Selby, a British management teacher, asks: "Do you know how to use silence to get people to talk?" He introduces people to interviewing with a list of OK questions, and another list of questions that are not OK. Managers in a consulting skills course might practice both kinds in role-playing. Selby lists four types of OK questions:

1. *The open question.* The interviewee has a choice in how he answers it. You can elicit more than one piece of information. In a selection interview, for example: "What do you think were the most important features of your last job?"

2. *The closed question.* This is to find out a specific

piece of information, often used as a follow-up to an open question. But it can be off-putting if you use it too often. In appraisal, for example: "What production target should we set for the next quarter?"

3. *The probe question*. You use this when you think the interviewee is evading or withholding something. For instance: "I take your point. But how often has fire drill actually been exercised during the past year?"

4. *The link question*. This leads on naturally from one topic to the next and sustains the flow of conversation. In a counseling interview, for example, you might use the following links: Q: "Where do you see yourself progressing now?" A: "Oh, I'd like to gain some variety in management experience." Q: "That's interesting. Have you thought about what kind of management education might help broaden your horizons?"

Selby's list of not-OK questions might be termed "Have you stopped beating your wife, and if not why not?" The first type of not-OK question is the double or multiple question that demands more than one answer. The interviewee gets confused, or forgets to answer parts of the question. In a grievance interview, for example: "What I want to get clear is who started the argument and why, and why didn't anybody do anything about it at the time?" Asked one at a time, these are more likely to elicit answers that make sense. The other no-no is the leading question that tells the interviewee the type of answer the interviewer wants to hear, or else lets him give a yes or no, without further information. In a disciplinary interview, for example, the parent/child voice intrudes: "You do understand then, don't you, the trouble your being late causes the whole department?"

Good types of interviews to use for practice in listening

are selection or counseling interviews, in which the purpose of the interviewer is simply to give the interviewee as much room as possible to reveal himself. A few guidelines can help in practice interviews:

1. **Relax the atmosphere.** Sort out the seating, the meeting place, and so on to put the interviewee at ease. (Some say face-to-face seating is more off-putting than side by side.) Avoid interruptions and distractions.

2. Even if you have advice to give, wait until he has done some talking first—and you have done some listening. He may give himself the same advice, in which case he is more likely to follow it.

3. Use open-ended questions and show real interest in the responses, following up as appropriate.

4. If he has a problem, try to get him to find his own solution.

5. Minimize criticism, even if you need to correct him in some way. Be constructive.

6. Don't talk down to him or make meaningless noises. Be clear in your own mind what you have to say, then be specific.

7. Be honest; don't pussyfoot around delicate bits. Make sure there is a clear outcome to the interview.

8. Keep limits to your time and emotional involvement and pay full attention within them. If you have only twenty minutes, say so at the beginning.

9. Note-taking may set up barriers with some people, while it reassures others; so ask first if you do it. Be patient if the interviewee is repetitious. Read the meta-messages and be prepared to probe tact-

fully, even if the topic is embarrassing to either of you.

10. Invite him to ask questions. This is particularly useful in a selection interview.

11. Confirm how well you've listened by summarizing what has been said and asking for comment.

12. If you didn't take notes during the interview, write it up immediately afterwards.

There are certain things that will close off any flow of information that has begun to open up. These include criticism, taking sides, showing bias, showing off, using jargon, and interrupting. If you let the interviewee divert you too easily into byways, that will also cut off useful information.

With a group of nurses, Selby used one technique that might be useful in any other course to train people in listening. He drew up three résumés of nursing managers and briefed three members of the course about them. Behind each résumé was another. One had a secret fiancé and was only looking for a short-term job. Another didn't have full qualifications in one required area but had enough other qualifications to mask the fact. The third had a very rigid personality and had been fired from one job. Then the class was broken into panels of four, who interviewed the "candidates" for a job. Surprisingly little of the background information emerged in the interviews—and members learned from their mistakes in the exercise.

Distance Lends Enchantment

No matter what his expertise, the greatest asset of the consultant is that he is a "stranger." He might be well known to the people he's listening to, but he is still not a member of their group. As is a marriage counselor, he is outside, so he doesn't have to take sides; he is disinterested but he isn't "not interested"; his objectivity comes from his distance from the person or group. Because of this distance, he is often given confidences that members of the group would not give each other. He is more free from ties of tradition and from emotion than members of the group. If he stays a long time with a group, this strangeness can be watered down, and a group can make him a full member, or nearly so, and in so doing they strip him of the one thing he has to offer them—his objectivity. Therefore, it is important that he remain accountable to someone outside the group; familiarity breeds membership.

To remain "strange," then, the in-house consultant needs to work fast. The earliest recognition and diagnosis will have a larger impact than later, more refined impressions, both on group members and perhaps on those above them. If he is not being used for specific expertise, then this approach, moving in and out of groups fairly rapidly, will give him credibility because each group can use him to measure themselves against the growing number of other groups with whom he has experience. "Yes, that's a fairly normal phenomenon," or "A lot of other groups have had this problem" can be comforting, so long as he avoids the "Miss Marple trap" of assuming that this group (and its problem) are exactly like those of other groups, thereby cutting off information about the group and the problem that may be vital. (Miss Marple in Agatha Christie's whodunits was always solving murders by noticing that so-and-so's eyes are too close together, just like the butcher boy's, and he used to steal lamb chops.)

One problem for the do-it-yourself consultant is divided loyalty. He remains accountable to someone outside (or upstairs) but the longer he stays (and the more polarized the problem) the more likely it is that he will side with the group, probably against those who brought him in, higher management. This can be useful to everyone if he is a capable advocate for the group, able to short-circuit hierarchy, but in the longer term it means he will be unpopular, probably in places where it can hurt his career. This is where he needs an umbrella held over him by someone (perhaps a mentor, or management developer) with enough power to protect him from temporary lapses in popularity.

Mirror, Mirror on the Wall . . .

There comes a time in every consultant's life when he has to pull his punches. Most of them, being ethical people, steeped in the art of letting it all hang out, of confrontation and feedback, of truth-telling, feel this is unethical. But if they tell the boss the truth, he'll boot them out. If they tell the group the whole truth, the shutters will come down, and again, their usefulness is at an end. So they soft-soap a little, feed out the nasty truth in sugar-coated doses.

That's quite OK. In fact, it's necessary. I even have academic "proof" (or at least a respectable citation) to back it up. Per-Olof Berg, studying a Swedish company in considerable depth, comes up with the OD-shattering notion that the important thing is to paint a picture that the *group* recognizes rather than to paint a picture that the consultant recognizes as true.

I have always believed that the role of the stranger, the consultant, was to hold up an objective mirror: "This is how you look from outside." But Berg's experience supports my own hard-learned observation that *their* recognition of themselves is more important than *my* impression of the truth.

Like the crone looking into her magic mirror (a good consultant until it began to chant Snow White's virtues), people want to see good reflections. "*You* are the fairest of all." Only in a context that matches their self-image (and a language that matches their patois) can the consultant suggest a small change here, or a potential problem there. Step by step, small symbol by small symbol, change by change, it is possible to develop quite major shifts in style, but only within the abilities of those who are watching themselves in the consultant's mirror to continue recognizing themselves. So it's not really a mirror at all, but a slightly abstract, pleasantly tinted painting, or sometimes simply a cartoon. The "medium" doesn't matter as much as the recognition —and it's the group's recognition, not the change agent's, so one's instincts in judging how and what they will recognize may matter more than one's intellect in giving a perfect diagnosis of their problems.

There are some shortcuts and tricks one can use to get them to paint the pictures themselves. In this sense the consultant or stranger is no longer a painter but simply the one supplying the paint to the participants.

At Ashridge Management College in England, a session on organization change often starts with the members "free-associating" on the word "organization." Most of the words that come back are negative: hierarchy, bureaucracy, rules, and so on. Then the leader asks the members: "Think of one organization you know which feels effective and tick the characteristics on this list [a long one] that match that organization." When they've done this, he then asks: "Do the same thing for an organization you know which feels ineffective." The characteristics they tick for the ineffective model are usually those of their own organization. But by describing the characteristics of what they feel is an effective organization, they have built their own model for the kind of organization they are trying to create. The picture is their own, and it helps them recognize the skills they'll need to build it in that model. If an exercise such as this, within a group that can actually implement some of the changes, is then presented by the group to higher management—again with some ability to make changes—it is possible to help the right things happen.

Similar tricks to help a group paint its own pictures come from other consultants. A can describe how B would describe A's strengths and weaknesses or motives; then B can do the same (whether A and B are individuals or groups); then they can be brought together to compare perceptions. The mirror from "them" is usually powerful in its matching parts as much as in its mismatches.

A very simple ploy, when a particular problem is being tackled, is to get members of the group together and have each one describe the problem, with the consultant writing down comments or elements or keywords on a blackboard as they go. This usually surfaces misconceptions or different conceptions and gives a problem-centered way of resolving them.

Another way of getting the participants to paint their own pictures is for the consultant to survey people's attitudes about the problem, then collate the results (thus assuring anonymity to all respondents) and feed them back to the group as a whole. This can be much less threatening than individual "interventions."

These approaches all stress the fact that the group is helping itself, with the consultant acting only as a facilitator or putting together a collage of their individual pictures. He promises no results and thus faces no inflated expectations. It may be more difficult to get across the self-help image in an environment in which people are accustomed to autocratic management. The main thing for the do-it-yourself consultant is that he is not the "doctor" serving up answers; he is simply a helper, oiling the team's problem-solving machinery.

Derek Sheane describes how it worked in three different examples: one of six managers of a unit of 1,500, one of an executive board managing 12,000, and one a new project team of fifteen designing and implementing a factory. Though the examples differed, he found each case involved six systematic steps, with the first five occurring within a few days at most:

1. *Contracting.* The consultant agrees on a "contract" with the head of the team. No matter who invites or suggests it, it is ultimately the boss who decides to go ahead and makes a contract with the consultant.

2. *Agreeing objectives.* The members of the team hear and agree what the objectives of the team-improvement activity are and how they'll be measured. He uses this stage to deal with the questions everyone has: Why are we doing this? Who is trying to do what to whom? What are the ground rules? This gives the consultant a chance to start building trust and credibility with team members he hasn't met.

3. *Data collection.* The consultant has individual discussions with each team member, listening to his worries, what he thinks important issues are, what needs to be done to improve teamwork. This also helps build trust in the consultant.

4. *Data analysis.* The consultant has to demonstrate highly credible intellectual understanding of what everyone said and classify it for sensible, jargon-free feedback in a "workable" way that gives the team a chance to see entry points for action.

5. *Feedback.* This is a two-stage thing, including diagnosis and action planning. The consultant presents the data he gathered from individuals, but not in a written report. Instead, he uses flip-charts and other visual aids that can be typed up later, when the group has amended them. This avoids individuals digging through written reports and focuses attention on a single picture. He thinks most issues will fit on two or three flip-charts. But the charts don't have the final conclusions; those are derived from the discussion. One team concludes: "The data indicate our four real priorities are . . ." This leads naturally to decisions as to what to do, in what order, by whom, and when.

6. *Review.* Later, a review meeting goes back over the action plan, looks at divergences, and moves on to further action.

Sheane also has a few more hints that are helpful. He suggests *using informal processes to create change*, gradually transforming all unhelpful, formal, and bureaucratic practices into informal processes—moving from formal committees to shirt-sleeve meetings on real issues, for example, or eliminating memos, or moving away from "information systems" to building networks. *Be pragmatic about power*, he says, including key decision-makers and informal opinion leaders in the process. "Power is the ability to do things; it is organized energy. Consequently, inclusion in decision-making should be pragmatic. Whether you 'approve' of an individual or group or not is irrelevant. If they have the power to influence outcomes then it is naive to exclude them." *Move to the open management of conflict*, he counsels: "Go out and seek 'bad news.'" If you confront problems early, they are more soluble. "An illness in its very early stages is hard to diagnose but easy to cure. An illness in its advanced stage is very easy to diagnose but much harder to cure." Finally, he says the consultant should *preach not only to the converted*. If you talk only to your friends you don't hear all the bad news. And if you don't keep lines open to some of the power figures who might block change, you may get a kind of groupish cold feet Sheane calls "ogre-building" in which people don't do things because "he" (sometimes "they") obviously wouldn't allow it, so why try?

Power and Politics

For a consultant who is also a member of an organization, the do-it-yourself approach is full of perils, real and imagined. His mentor must be prepared to protect him on occasion but not to buffer him from some rough treatment. As every consultant learns, the client usually wants a "solution" (preferably yesterday) to a clearly specified problem, whereas the consultant usually presents a "process" to tackle a much more basic, deep-seated problem. Here again, the client's recognition may be more important than the consultant's realistic picture. When it actually comes to implementing the process, the client often wants to start superficially and more slowly, and the consultant usually wants to barge ahead at full speed. The do-it-yourself consultant, dealing with power figures in his own organization, may avoid some traps that bedevil outside consultants by heeding the gently-gently messages and even by pulling his punches in diagnosis, so long as he retains a license to carry on helping change happen at an organic pace.

If there are natural "consulting" groups in a company they sometimes get into conflicts with each other, a factor that can be used to "manage" them. Pettigrew describes a medium-size company whose board of directors encourages such conflict in order to control consultant groups:

> By keeping distant from the scene of conflict, by giving the programmers some freedom from the system of bureaucratic rules, and by keeping job assignments uncertain, subject to change at any moment, they prevented the programmers from consolidating in a stable power base, and still managed to extract the work necessary for the company's continued prosperity.

Power figures can (and often do) use the consultant as a scapegoat, blaming him for decisions which are necessary but bound to be unpopular. This is easier to avoid if the consultant sidesteps the trap of recommending solutions and expresses only what the group itself has decided. On the other hand, the in-house consultant gains another kind of power, as Bailey points out:

> Knowledge is power. The man who correctly understands how a particular structure works can prevent it from working or make it work differently with much less effort than a man who does not know these things.

Finally, let me cite Jack Grayson at a 1979 management conference: "Every organization contains the finest possible consultants: its own staff."

Chapter 22.

DEVELOPMENT AND EDUCATION

In my private lexicon, "management education" is something relatively formal that happens outside the company, and "management development" happens inside, often quite informally. But these are not mutually exclusive terms any more than they are mutually exclusive happenings. Ideally, the growth of a good manager should have elements that are outside *and* inside, formal *and* informal. It's the yin/yang idea again, with each part complementary to the other.

What happens to the manager whose entire growth has occurred inside the company, with no formal "program"? He is as likely as anyone else to grow into a good manager— but a little less likely than someone who has been in contact with managers from other companies to know what a good manager he is. So the contribution of management education that may be most important is the confidence it may give its participants—mainly by rubbing shoulders with one another.

What happens to the well-groomed manager who is sent through a highly programmed sequence of courses, without enough chance to develop inside the company? He's likely to know all the concepts, and this may indeed give him confidence, but he'll be hampered in dealing with less-schooled people because his language and ways of thinking will be too academic. And he'll be hampered in using some of the concepts because the ease that comes with practice will be missing, and the ability to adapt the concept to the circumstances comes only with use. So the contribution of management development that is most important is the pragmatism and people skills its participants develop—mainly through contact with the real world.

Dive in the Deep End

My research into management education in the past few years has convinced me that the most important aspects in the growth of a manager are those that happen at work, especially in his first few years of work. It's analogous to the growth of a child; the influences in the first two years are far more important than anything that happens at school, or during the school years—but we wouldn't do away with schooling because of that! The "infant" manager, given a good mentor and lots of opportunities to dive in the deep end and learn to swim, will grow, no matter what other educational experiences are later overlaid. I know one fine manager who says his entire career can be attributed to his first boss—who was about to fire him from his first management job but fell ill, and the fledgling manager had to step into his shoes for a few months and *manage*. He did it well and became in his own eyes and soon in the eyes of others one of the best in the business. If that superior had remained at work one more week the young man's entire career would probably have been blighted by a sense of failure and a fear of further failure. That's how bureaucrats are made.

I also know managers whose careers were "made" by an experience in management education. Although teachers would like to think their inputs make the difference, the truth is that the earth-shattering experience, especially for a manager who has spent ten years or more inside a single firm, is often simply finding out that he can hold his own as well as his peers on a course.

"More than half of what I learned came in the coffee breaks." That's what dozens of managers have said after attending formal courses. (The "coffee breaks" often include the after-hours sessions, some of which go on into very small hours, without benefit of academic clergy.) Although it is human nature to want some spoon-feeding in the form of formal lectures, in my view the function of the lectures, games, case studies, and all the other things that appear in the formal curriculum is largely to get the members of a course sufficiently limbered up that they can talk freely to each other in the moments when they think they are "goofing off.". It is the spaces between the formal portions that give them confidence, insight, chances to measure their own experience and re-evaluate it, and chances to learn from the experience of others they are learning to respect.

It is, in this context, far more important to evaluate the choice of members for a course than it is to measure the competence of the teachers, or the actual content of what they teach. As long as course members regard one another as peers and as long as a course group "welds," then the members will take home some insight, learning, and confidence without respect to the teaching. If a fast-track young tiger is let loose in a course of old workhorses, he may shut them up, and they may close him out, and everyone loses a little. Similarly, if people from vastly different backgrounds are dumped together in a course that is top-heavy with instruction and lacking in chances to pierce the language barriers among the student body, then the members may never weld into a unit and may not learn as much from one another as they could.

Action Learning

There are certain approaches to formal management education that give better-than-average chances for groups to weld and members to learn from one another. One of my favorites goes by the name of "action learning," the brainchild more than twenty-five years ago of an eccentric English professor by the name of Reg Revans. Although he was able to use the basic idea of managers learning with and from each other in several British organizations, it was not until 1967 in Brussels that he was able to use action learning in a formal management education context.

In action learning, a group of about four to six managers is assigned, part or full time, to work on major problems. They may be individual problems or a single group problem; they can be in the manager's own organization or in some entirely different function or industry.

Revans originally contended that part of the learning came from being in a foreign culture—an idea with which I heartily agree. I am also sympathetic with people who must undertake the risk of doing something new and untested inside their own companies, especially if they have to carry on doing their normal tasks at the same time. But experience has shown that whether the task is individual or shared, at home or away, in one's own field or in a foreign speciality, the learning depends much more on how well the group welds, and to what extent its members believe action will occur as the result of their efforts.

One of the most effective forms of action learning I have encountered, initiated by John Morris at Rolls-Royce, goes by the name of "Joint Development Activity" ("JDA"). In the JDA pattern a few people from a company are assigned full time for a few months to work on a single problem central to the company's future—such as a new product line or a complete reorganization or how to bring in computers. Given close and frequent contact with a top-level steering group, the JDA participants do their fact-finding, analysis, and presentations and go beyond recommendations to implementing their plans. So it is with action learning in general—and it is usually so effective in the problem-solving realm that some companies use it as a form of in-house consulting, almost forgetting the initial reason for its development: the growth of future top managers.

Action learning is a "formal" management education activity, in use at a growing number of European institutions, because a growing number of management teachers recognize the shortcomings of the chalk-and-talk approaches they have inherited from the university tradition. Quite a few *like* the role of helper or facilitator that action learning thrusts upon the "set advisor." They also like the adult relationships among set members, advisors, and other experts the sets choose to bring in.

Most action-learning activities start with a residential period, •often including the higher-ups who "own" the problems, to· sort out priorities, reporting lines, resources available (including the time of the participants), and the expectations of everyone involved. This is important, because the problems often grow (as do-it-yourself consultants learn quickly), and clients are not always happy with broad redefinitions of formerly tidy problems. Then set members get together in their fours or sixes, usually once a week for at least half a day (and preferably the night before, for informal activities together), to report progress to one another and co-consult about their problems or difficulties on shared problems. In due course, they usually realize they need to learn more about statistics or interviewing skills or accounting or some other special subject, and the set advisor, acting as a kind of educational "broker," finds the expert who can do the best and fastest job of bringing the members up to par on the subject they have pinpointed. Thus, the lecture content is completely under control of the "students," and they tend to wring any visiting expert dry once they've decided they need his know-how.

The key to action learning is that the "laboratory" is a real working situation; the guinea pigs are real people, and the results are real profits and losses and organizational situations. There is no "play" or "role-play" or written case study in this. Each member with his problem is a walking, talking, moving case study, and every other member cares about him and therefore his "case" in a way no case-study class could ever care about the best-written case. If information they feel is necessary is missing, he can go get it, and they all learn the implications of asking questions that might raise expectations in an organization. The politics of situations, so often missing in formal management education, are implicit in the real-world problems. There is personal risk and accountability for the participants—but there is also an emotional support system in the form of their fellow members, who are undergoing similar risks.

I am devoted to action learning and its variations because they combine learning, exposure to others from outside cultures, informal shoulder-rubbing, and so on, with the best of management development, in the form of risk-taking, accountability, and access to older, wiser managers who can share their insights about organizations and sometimes hold slightly protective umbrellas over developing managers.

Management Monasteries

But what of those business schools, management centers, technical colleges, and other erudite centers of management education, pointed at everything from the eighteen-year-old lad with some notion he might be interested in business, to the second-career pre-retirement student in his fifties? Are they unnecessary luxuries, all those classrooms and buildings and grounds? I don't think so, as long as we use them wisely.

Just as we need approaches that use the business itself as a laboratory, so we also need serene islands *away* from the business, where managers can get a different perspective once in a while. We also need mechanisms to find potential young tigers and expose them to the business culture before they have to make life decisions. It helps when we can put a lot of them under one roof and let them strike sparks off each other (though success or failure at business school is not necessarily the mark of potential business successes—and indeed, a B school may be off-putting to some of our more entrepreneurial young people). We also need academic institutions to serve as the intellectual yang, as counterpoint to the pragmatic yin of day-to-day business. The concepts that develop in business schools often come from good observations by their good thinkers—observations *in* business.

The ideas of McGregor and Herzberg and Likert are based on such observations, but it was the academic milieu that gave the conceptualizers time and reason to find patterns that the rest of us might have missed. And it is the academic environment that values such concepts and moves them around effectively (provided there are translators who can express the academic concepts about business in pragmatic language and examples).

I have a suspicion of single-technique business schools because they become trapped in their own innovations. The "case method" was a magnificent improvement on traditional academic lectures in that it allowed young people to be exposed to hundreds of examples of business within a single year or two. But slavish adherence to only the case method cuts out many other techniques by which they might explore other nuances of business behavior—and the case is only as good as the eye and pen of the observer who wrote it. Those courses that point themselves at experienced managers and concentrate on welding them into "syndicates" of six to twelve seem to do well, whatever potpourri of techniques they use, because the managers have a chance to learn from one another informally, as well as learning formally in the classroom. (And in truth, I think the function of the classroom for experienced managers is simply to oil the machinery for the informal learning—an heretical view that will not endear me to many fine teachers.) The T-group or any other behavioral course that is sold widely and thus attracts people from many different corporate cultures will have the benefit of contact—but may limit it only to the psyches of the members or interrelationships between them at the cost of some of their more down-to-earth experience.

In other words, those "courses" that tap into the live "cases" of the participants and those that let the participants weld into useful small groups seem to be most effective. One more aspect may bear mentioning again: if managers are sent on courses in pairs or trios from the same department or activity, they have a better chance of riding out inevitable re-entry shock and carrying into practice some of what they learned while they were away. The confidence-giving aspects of getting away into stranger groups *can* be combined with the shared-experience aspects of going away in family groups, but only with a bit of forethought and recognition of the benefits of both.

Business as a Laboratory

Business schools can be useful in another way, and business can be useful to management education at the same time. If the business is viewed as the laboratory, then why not view managers as learners in conjunction with outsiders who would benefit from coming in to study business problems. What I am suggesting is a team approach to management research, in which the company with a problem and the academic with a special interest can combine forces in a win/win game. Not every academic institution is yet prepared to encourage such approaches, but the academic who has access to inside information and insiders working alongside him on the problem will learn more himself and may contribute more to management knowledge in the long run. And the "post-graduate" managers working with him (who may, indeed, be able to gain higher degrees if their research is sufficiently rigorous) will not only learn, but will also be able to help the company implement solutions to its problem. This would fit into an existing form of research called "action research" which already stresses the importance of feeding back findings into a company and thus influencing its progress (as opposed to the pure academic model, in which the researcher is not supposed to influence the process he is studying).

One of the most important uses of business and management education may be a form of "brokerage," with the educator acting as broker between the organization that has a problem and other academics who have specific know-how or insight or fact-finding abilities that particularly suit the problem. It is likely that this "networking" approach to management education will become much more common in the future. Already most leading business schools have a few teachers who prefer to work this way, and I believe their number is growing.

Chapter 23.

MANAGERS AND MENTORS

The best way to get ahead in management is to get yourself a mentor. Many managers have known this instinctively and gone about it instinctively for decades. Today the idea is gaining formal popularity. It used to be a slightly shameful approach, with a "teacher's pet" flavor about it, but most managers recognized the phenomenon of "drafting," riding along behind a winner, picking up some of his momentum, or sucked along in his air currents, like a racing driver.

Managers with mentors get ahead in their organizations faster than those without, and they also, in turn, have more protégés themselves. Thus, the organization that encourages a mentor approach to management development wins in more than one generation of management.

What is this magic "mentor" that adds momentum to a manager's career? He need not be a "winning" manager himself. In fact, many managers at the sharpest rising curves of their own careers do not have the patience and sensitivity to watch over the careers of younger people; these may, indeed, regard rising younger stars as threats. So the ideal mentor is more likely to be older, content with his own place in the organization—an "uncle" figure rather than a powerful father or ambitious big brother. He is the one to whom the young manager can go with questions about the policies and practices in the organization, and he is also the one with the unwritten folklore, the myths, the canons of the faith, and the commandments at his fingertips. "If you can back up your case with facts, it's best to argue with the president on this one." Or, conversely, "Young managers should be seen but not heard in the executive dining room."

In this way, alone, a mentor can speed the full membership of a young manager in the organization. One study at a British management center was pointed at finding out what newly appointed supervisors needed to know in their first weeks and months as managers. These people, usually just off the shop-floor, had been neglected for some years, and a number of companies were beginning to ask for supervisor-development courses. The management center decided that rather than putting together a tidy package of modules ("communication skills," "financial fluency," and so on) immediately, they ought to go out and find out what life was like for a first-time supervisor. The results were surprising. The new supervisor may, indeed, need some finance or communications skills in the long run; but his first problems have much more to do with the management culture of the organization. "How in Hades do I cope with this mountain of forms?" "Am I expected to go to the weekly review meetings now?" "Who do I go to with this kind of grievance?" "How can I get the production director to pay serious attention to this problem?" There isn't a course in the world, no matter how cleverly modular, that can help with this kind of question. What the new supervisors needed was a little organizational hand-holding. So the management center turned its attention to potential sources of the organizational know-how and winkled out some potential mentors in the same firms and then put together a short course in coaching and counseling skills for them. The results were very gratifying, both to the new mentors and the new supervisors. (With this kind of credibility, the management center was also able to peddle its modular supervisor course very soon thereafter.)

For a manager "over the hill" being a mentor can actually enrich a job that may be beginning to feel stale and sterile. He may feel that his wisdom about the company is wasted, that few appreciate how useful his contributions can be. (Few managers are rewarded for *avoiding* problems—only solving them—so the wise old manager who can sidestep difficulties often feels underappreciated.)

Marjo Von Boeschoten, a leading European change agent, draws a "learning curve" of a typical manager's life. He probably plays win/lose games in his twenties and thirties, and because he is young and energetic, he probably wins, so his learning is high. Somewhere around forty, though, he has

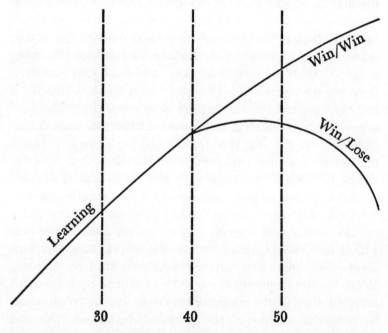

to make a vital choice. If he goes on playing win/lose games, he will inevitably begin losing some, and this will drive him into more and more defensive postures; his learning quotient will begin to drop, and the vicious circle continues. On the other hand, if he re-evaluates his approach (or if it has been a win/win approach all along) and begins to get some of his wins from developing the skills and wisdom of younger people, he not only goes on winning through their wins, he also goes on learning. He stays turned on. He goes on being needed. And his contributions to the organization, whether they are appreciated or not, go on increasing.

Many young managers naturally find mentors for themselves. Early in my career I had two; both were my superiors at the time but they remained mentors much longer. We maintained the links for our own reasons, not those of a company. (I changed companies more often than my mentors did.) For me, they had more wisdom and support to contribute, and I liked being around them. For them, I think watching my growth and development was rewarding. Now, almost eighteen years after our first encounter, I am still happily in touch with the man who gave me my first responsible job.

Many natural mentors find protégés for themselves. They simply work in a development way and have a natural affinity for good raw material. My mentor can tell me what happened to most of the other people I was working with in the early sixties, and he takes pride in their careers.

In other words, plenty of capable individuals will take care of themselves on the mentor front. My concern is for companies who are wasting resources and for potential mentors or protégés who have not given the matter any thought—and who will not learn enough or do quite as well as a result.

The company that moves people around rapidly, for example, is probably giving its young managers plenty of opportunities for risk and recognition. But it may be whirling them too fast to develop lasting relationships with potential mentors, thus depriving both parties as well as the company of more development opportunities. If a coaching or counseling relationship can be established at the beginning of a young manager's career and somehow maintained for a few years, no matter how he moves, I think he'll do better, and so will his mentor. In formal terms, the mentor may be the one who decides you're ready to be thrown in the deep end, who then throws you a pair of water wings, or fishes you out when you start floundering. Informally, he's a source of wisdom. I believe there's a case for combining the two at the beginning and retaining the voice of the mentor in the young manager's career assignments for as long as it suits them both. So in this model the mentor has to have a certain amount of power or persuasion, reaching beyond his specific assigned area of responsibility.

One large company has a concept that can help in this kind of situation. When a young manager is sent away on assignment, whether it be two months or two years, he has a "career manager" in addition to his old and new line managers. This is the mentor, but he is held accountable for the younger manager's well-being, the smoothness of his move, whether he stays in touch with the home group and its happenings, whether an appropriate post is waiting for him on his scheduled return, and how graceful his re-entry is. The strict accountability, part of that company's culture, may not be necessary in building mentor relationships into fast-moving careers, but it probably helps emphasize the importance of the relationship and of retaining links to the "home" part of the organization.

I've talked to a number of managers who say the most profound influence in their early years was not a mentor but an anti-mentor (or "tor-mentor"), a manager who was so difficult, or autocratic, that the young manager would do almost anything to get promoted out of his orbit, or would take the opposite approach or style in most of his subsequent dealings with people.

Remembering the young manager whose "mentor" was the man who was about to fire him, I recognize that capable young people will usually find ways to learn. But this man says that if his boss hadn't fallen sick, his career would have been much less spectacular. Leaving organizational survival to the fittest may waste human and corporate resources and deprive some people of a sense of fitness they need in order to go on growing. If the ability to find mentors and develop mentor relationships is built into the early stages of careers, the chances of such waste are reduced, and the chances of growth are increased. It's a win/win game.

Chapter 24.

VISIBILITY AND ACCOUNTABILITY

The day before their graduation, I had lunch with a group of MBA candidates at the London Business School, one of Europe's best management education emporia. The six young tigers and tigresses, an international group with considerable management experience before they started, were discussing their various job offers.

"Why did you accept the offer from X, Dennis? I thought Y offered more money and a better-sounding position," I asked.

"But X has a great reputation for developing people," he answered. The rest nodded and started a list of the companies that had that kind of reputation among the elite would-be managers. I found quite a few names I hadn't heard before. I asked another why he was going to one of these "unknown" companies.

"It's simple," he answered. "They're teaming me with a great guy who has an MBA from Stanford, and we're going to be developing a product of our own. We'll stand or fall on how well we do it." The company had been hiring MBAs for only a few years but it had learned how to use the drive and energy of the young tigers and what turns them on.

In almost every case, today's ambitious young people will choose opportunity over status, risk over security, visibility over membership. Of this half-dozen, not one wanted to go into a "management training program." What they wanted were projects of their own, new ventures, lots of movement, and loose enough organizations that they could try to make their marks.

"I've been 'processed' long enough," said one. "It's time to get out and do something for myself." He intended to do it under the aegis of a company, not completely on his own, but at the back of his mind was the idea that he would probably want to start his own business after spending a few years learning on the ground how other people run theirs.

The MBA is one breed of young tiger, readying himself for an ambitious career in business, whether his own or someone else's. He has already invested time and money in his own development, and his expectations, though they may be slightly inflated for his years, will drive him for quite a few years. A company that recognizes and channels that motivation will probably get its money's worth.

Another breed of young tiger is less visible but perhaps just as important. As Gail Sheehy points out, many young people defer the "who-am-I?" decision as long as possible, well into their early twenties. A company that takes in able people and gives them chances to explore their own capabilities will find that a certain percentage of them take hold and begin to grow themselves in specific directions—to everyone's benefit.

A company is not just a finishing school for young tigers, though. It is an institution that makes things (including money). Young tigers and their development can be a nuisance if their implicit demands detract from the primary goals of the organization, or its *modus vivendi*. However, I find there is a strong correlation between companies that consistently make money and those that consistently develop young managers. So for the sake of companies as well as young tigers, we ought to explore how they do it.

Many companies have formal management development programs, but the ones I find most successful at it have something more important: an approach that gives the fledgling manager plenty of opportunity to try his wings. "I'm going to XYZ because I'll be able to run a factory of my own within eighteen months," says one of the young tigers at lunch. "By the time I was twenty-eight I was on an elite project team designing an entirely new plant on a green-field site," says an older manager. "I was only twenty-six when they gave me the Des Moines office to run," says a computer executive.

If the earliest experiences are the most important, then it seems wasteful to put able young people in positions where they can't make mistakes, where they have no responsibility —no matter how much "learning" is spoon-fed to them in the process. We have ample evidence that people who reach the tops of companies spend relatively little time in their middles; instead, they are likely to be out "on their own" in company terms, with chances to win or lose. If an ambitious young person "loses" in some such early experience, he can go on learning, and wise companies have ways to keep these people and keep them growing. The confident "loser" will go on, either there or somewhere else, and try again. The one who has not yet gained self-confidence may subside into mediocrity, and he's the one who will spend the rest of his career in the middle, probably in the company where he started. This is where the combination of mentors and individual accountability—and visible recognition—comes into play. "Give them enough rope . . ." might be the watchword for the company's entire approach to management development, but it may be the role of the mentor to play out the rope at the right times, or to extend lifelines when a young manager is in danger of getting in over his head. It may also be the role of the mentor to encourage the more fainthearted beginner to take more risk, to find some other way than "playing it safe." I believe the majority of managers can grow and learn and take responsibility and live up to it if they are given enough chances to do so early enough.

Visibility is important, recognition for one's achievements. At the same time, the early development depends on "punishments" being sufficiently mild and bearable that normal people will go on trying. When a four-year-old first wants mobility, you give him a tricycle, not a Chevrolet. You stand by with Band-Aids and patch up his skinned knees as he learns to ride, and you try to keep him from running into the Chippendale too often. Later, when he wants a bike, you make sure he's careful and canny about traffic, and you prepare yourself to chauffeur the battered bike to the repair shop now and then as he learns what he can and can't do with it. A few years later, he has a mentor as he learns to steer and control a car, and he isn't set loose with it until he has had formal training, both in how it works and what the rules are governing its use, and informal practice, with some gentle opportunities to bump into curbs or wooden barriers.

Management is equally complex and requires a similar mix of intellect and instinct, and you don't get the instinctive reactions built into your autonomic nervous system until you've had those opportunities to make mistakes.

A number of companies have "A lists" of young managers who have been identified as having particularly high potential. These people usually get enriched opportunities to try their wings. They are moved around faster, counseled more often, sent on more courses, and have the best possible chances to acquire mentors, organizational know-how, and a sense of opportunity.

The trouble with this approach is that it often creates a "crown-prince syndrome." Those who are on the A list (and most people usually know who they are, no matter how secret the list) may gain extra confidence from the knowledge. But others who realize they are *not* on the list for special treatment may be turned off, demotivated, and thereby wasted. In one big chemical company managers say: "If you don't have a star on your forehead by the time you're twenty-seven, you'll never make it to top management, no matter *how* good you are. There are simply too many other good contenders, so you have to get noticed early." In that company, though, almost *every* young manager has opportunities to run his own show, or take part in some new and risky activity. The management development approach stretches across the board, and the crown princes tend to emerge in a fairly organic way.

No matter what we say about demotivating the others, every company does have crown princes, and they do get special treatment. One approach the chemical company uses is a kind of "recycling" course for those who are *not* among the elite, a chance for the normal, garden-variety manager to sit back and look at the issues that affect jobs, and his job, and to feel that the company values him enough to send him away for a week or so, fairly regularly. Paired with a corporate culture that values the middle managers fairly highly and pays them well, this seems to result in "backbone" managers who are more turned on than average. Another element that may help in their continued growth is fairly widespread encouragement to make rather drastic changes in career—from technical to general, or production to personnel—at every level, not just the entry stage.

"Learning by doing" is the watchword. The learning is for most people a reward in its own right; the reward system can be further enhanced in several important ways:

* Giving recognition to those who succeed notably. This need not mean giving them more pay, simply mentioning them in important meetings or sending them off to conferences or other gatherings away from their home sites or encouraging others with similar tasks to consult them as experts.

* Bailing out those who are getting in trouble but making sure they have plenty of opportunity to discuss the problems and learn from any mistakes; this means they need contact with counseling figures rather than power figures.

* Teaming those who are taking on new tasks with others whom they can consider as peers. A "co-con-

/ 235

sulting" group, welded properly, learns more and is rewarded better by the interest, concern, and support of the peers.

If the system has sufficient humanity to develop people in this way, using the visibility of their endeavors and accountability for their mistakes, then it will also have a Darwinian element—the ability to keep hands off when things are going well, or even when they may be stumbling a little. This takes judgment on the part of mentors but adds immeasurably to the sense of accountability. The fittest are seen to survive and thrive and to do it all by themselves.

Chapter 25.

SELF-DEVELOPMENT

Who "owns" a manager? In the best interests of the employer as well as the individual, I think he should own himself. This means that he (or she) is ultimately in charge of his (or her) own development, without respect to management development systems and management education institutions, whether it takes place at work or in a Tuesday-night pottery class, or exchanging ideas with a friend at a Sunday barbecue.

Any of us, reviewing our own learning, would recognize the yin and yang elements. Some things we learn almost accidentally; two ideas bump into each other at the right time, and we're off on a new tack. Some things we decide we want to learn, then we pursue them until we feel we've learned enough about them. I am concerned that the institutions (schools, universities, management colleges, etc.) that dispense formal education and the qualifications (or "wallpaper") that go with it show very little recognition of either the accidental element or the self-managed element. It is the individual's decisions regarding what he wants to learn, and why, and how he wants to learn it, and how much of it he wants to learn that should be the pacing items, not the requirements for prerequisites and course-points and curriculum convenience of the institution.

Similarly, the company-sponsored management development program that leans heavily on the formal content to the detriment of the accidental or self-programmed elements is losing out, not only in the attention and motivation of the managers it processes, but also in the quality of managers it can ultimately attract and retain.

An individual who is caught up in the toils of such systems has every right to augment his learning in different ways, or to rebel if too much is being spoon-fed and too little self-driven. There are *always* alternatives, whether they be schools, bosses, employers, or courses. The alternatives always carry a cost, be it financial, emotional, or social, but they exist and are within the individual's span of discretion to explore and develop.

Self-Managed Learning

An English management center has taken this approach to considerable lengths, spurred on by a trend to "self-managed learning" that is growing rapidly in Europe. It started in an undergraduate college with what might be termed a "truck-driver's degree." An individual of any age or station in life who wanted to explore further education could come into the college (at any time of the year, not just on some magic "registration day" in September) and discuss his interests and needs. If he went into the program he would spend quite a few hours with a tutor, considering where he's been, where he is now, where he wants to go, how he gets there, and how he's going to know if he's arrived. In the process, he develops a pretty good inventory of the skills and knowledge and experience and personality he's starting with, and another picture of the bits he wants to add and how to add them. Finally, he knows how his learning will be measured—by the college as well as by himself, but to criteria he's decided for himself.

The new "student" is then teamed with a few others, often doing quite different things. One might be studying Irish history and Gaelic language, and farming techniques (his uncle is going to leave him a farm in County Kerry), while another is moving from the shop-floor into a personnel job with a lot of union history, sociology, and some business courses, and a third is studying group behavior and modern art, and care of retarded children. But the group members spend half a day with one another every week, reporting on the progress of their independent studies.

The tutor in this arrangement has several tasks. He is an individual mentor for the people over whom he watches and also a "broker," finding for them among the seven hundred faculty members those who know just exactly what the students want to know. It might be one or two lectures here, a once-a-week course there, a couple of tutorial hours with another expert, and so on. With a population of that many teachers, the tutor works through a network of people in the different major departments who know their own resources well. The tutor is also the facilitator or catalyst for the student group, helping it weld together and to get over any hurdle. (Those are most likely to occur if the group members are not well matched in basic abilities, or if one member gets into prolonged difficulties at the expense of time the others might be spending on themselves and one another.)

After a year or so of individual work and team-reporting, the student is usually able to produce some tangible evidence of his learning. A girl who met a photographer in Corfu might, for example, learn enough modern Greek to interview villagers about their lives, and enough sociology, Greek history, and ecology to evaluate their situation, and then develop enough writing skill to do the text for the photographer's book about the effects of tourism on a single Corfu village. The book might be her "thesis," after which she is admitted to the normal portion of the college for a final year of normal courses that qualify her for a degree. As a means of attracting many kinds of self-directed but not necessarily formally qualified people into further education, it clearly works, and as a means of educating them in the true sense of the word, it also works. The focus is the person who is learning, not the subject that is being learned.

This approach moved very easily into management education (by one of its founders moving into an associated management center, of course). Ian Cunningham is now operating a self-managed learning center that is portable as well as learner-centered. He is able to go out into a gathering or into a company with a certain number of books, filmstrips, bibliographies, and do-it-yourself tests and deal with groups of people, but on an individual basis. He can, for example, find out what elements of people's jobs they think are most important and what skills those parts of their work require, and then help them test themselves across a variety of skills and interests. Those skills that are most important in their jobs and in which the managers are less than proficient can then be the focus for further action; and he says it is possible within a single day to make enough progress to encourage people into further development.

This works only when the people themselves want to learn. If the tests ("instruments," as the experts call them) have pre-determined best answers, or are felt to coerce in any way those taking them, they will be viewed as just another example of manipulation from on high. Only when the values are those of the person taking the little tests, and the choices are his own as a result, does real self-managed learning follow such an exercise. There is useful learning, too, just in becoming aware of what you really need to learn about.

John Burgoyne, the guru of self-managed learning in Europe, has set out four factors that seem to be necessary conditions for this approach to learning:

* The learner is viewed as an "agent," not a "patient."

* The process is relatively responsive to the learner.

* He initiates it.

* He is able to learn independently, choosing his own pace, as well as the kinds of things he wants to do.

Courses for Horses

Different people learn in different ways, and one man's meat can be another's poison. My own learning comes through some process of eye-hand coordination; if I'm reading a book I underline the text; if I'm listening to a lecture I take voluminous notes. I may never have to refer to them again, but the process of taking them seems to put the information into my core storage in a useful way. Sometimes I can retrieve whole paragraphs almost intact; I "see" them in my mind's eye and simply read them off some kind of screen. But the things that touch the other portion of my brain, the ones that affect my emotions, tend to come via my ears—the timbre of a voice or a particular chord or a sense of urgency I hear in what would on the surface seem mundane comments. I have a friend who is the other way around. To learn, or to take things into the logical, "yang" portion of his brain, he needs to hear them. Cassettes and films and lectures are his medium; but the things he feels most poignantly come through his eyes—a sunset, a painting, a poem. What he wanted from me were letters; what I wanted from him were phone calls; for years we were slightly at cross-purposes, until we realized what was awry.

Most people, left to their own devices with a range of choices, will consciously or subconsciously choose the ways that suit them best; and if someone shares my yin/yang difference in input media for learning or feeling, he will probably choose the medium that fits the needs that are paramount at the moment. Sometimes we want to "learn" and sometimes we want to "feel"; both are part of the overall process of development.

Most formal courses dispense information in the medium that suits the skills of the teacher or the culture of the institution, without much regard for individual differences in the students. If there is a good fit, the manager/student will probably like the content of the course and learn a good deal from it; if the fit is awkward, he may still benefit from contact with his peers and from certain ideas that get through anyway, but he is more likely to be impatient and perhaps less likely to come away with as much confidence.

An individual's learning can be increased considerably if the implied contract between himself and his employer—which occurs every time he is sent on a course—is made more explicit. If it is possible to extend the "contract" discussions to those who are in charge of management education (whether they be inside the firm or outside), still further gains are possible.

If a person doesn't want to learn something, it's useless to send him on a course. And some people who profess the desire for training are not looking for learning as much as for credentials. So the first step in making a contract is finding ways for the individual to spell out what he consciously *does* want, and why. This is more difficult than it sounds in many organizations; if you ask people on the first day of any outside course why they are there, about 70 percent will say: "My company sent me," and shrug their shoulders. They're accustomed to going, sometimes slightly pleased, because being sent outside is usually viewed as some kind of accolade, though some worry that the cause is more likely to be remedial: "I suppose I'm here because I don't know enough about finance." This step amounts to making a contract with *himself*, and the job of a mentor or advisor or superior or personnel person is simply to help him spell it out and perhaps test any assertions ("What if . . . ?") that don't quite ring true.

Making a contract with the company sometimes takes the help of an outsider, because companies are not yet accustomed to people wanting two-way expectations spelled out in the learning realm. The word "negotiation" is usually reserved for pay and conditions and carries a connotation of potential conflict, but this is, in truth, another kind of negotiation, and both can benefit from it, even if the only difference is greater awareness of the subterranean expectations on both sides. More important, spelling it out can increase the expectations and help both parties live up to them.

Philip Boxer has developed a "course" for managers in a single company that rests upon this contracting idea. Working with outside tutors, the five or six managers embarking on a six-month project-based venture first of all work out what they want from it and then discuss with senior executives what the company expects. But one basic tenet of Boxer's faith is that the company will promise to the participants all the room they need to make changes, to do things differently. This sounds perilous for the firm, but as it works out, the contract puts the onus on the person: "We're promising to cut out the organizational and bureaucratic stumbling blocks, and you're promising to change things." Excuses for not doing things are suddenly removed; the contract constitutes a formal "license" to do things and learn from the experience. The individual is forced to examine some of the assumptions and hesitations inside himself as he gets into the program. Another contract exists between the outsiders and the company: if the participants do not report complete satisfaction with the course, the company has to pay only 25 percent of the fees for the outsiders. The participants know about this contract, too, from the beginning.

Most "contracts" about learning today are one way: "We're sending you on this course and we expect better performance in this respect or that as a result." Seldom does a company take on itself responsibility for giving people room to practice what has been preached, or even time to think about it or share the experience with others when they return. By making the process explicit and two way (or preferably three way, with expectations clarified with the educators as well), the company can actually gain a great deal, and so can the individual. The more he is actually and emotionally directing his own development, the better he is likely to develop.

Chapter 26.

FATHERS AND HUSBANDS

The stereotype of the man at the top is all wrong. Traditionally, he is pictured as a cold fish, distant from his children, neglectful of his doting wife, a workaholic with few friends, too busy for avocations and relationships. The truth is beginning to emerge today. Evidence shows that he is actually *more* likely to have a good relationship with his wife, to be closer to his children, to have warmer friendships and more interesting outside activities than the manager who didn't get to the top.

Getting there, on the other hand, is a less salubrious process, more in keeping with the stereotypes. It is in the middle ranges of management and in the early, striving years that people have trouble balancing the demands of home and family and the demands—or achievements—of work.

Professor Edgar Schein at MIT has noted an interesting yin/yang balance in managers, compared to other professions. He found that scientists and academics are highly involved in work, and their family involvement is quite low. Engineers are the reverse, with high family involvement and low work involvement. But the managers he studied were exceptionally high on *both* family and work involvement. They really care, in both worlds.

What they *do* about it is another matter. Fernando Bartolomé and Paul Lee Evans at INSEAD studied more than five hundred managers from a number of countries and interviewed a number of wives as well. The managers were fairly well balanced in their concern and involvement with work and home—but work won in both time and energy when it came to how they invest themselves. They spent nearly three times the energy on their jobs and twice as much time; the wives agreed with their husbands' estimates within a point or two, incidentally.

There's an emotional imbalance, too, that supports the stereotype of the tired husband coming home and taking out his work worries on the wife and children. Most of the managers admitted their minds were often on other things when their wives and children talked to them in the evening, and many felt guilty about this. No one but the researchers dared suggest that a manager with worries about his home life would ever take them out on his boss in the morning! One husband said explicitly: "If I'm miserable on the job, I'll be miserable at home. The converse would not be true."

Almost half the managers said they were unhappy about their current life-styles and wanted to improve them. This meant improving both the quantity—the amount of time available to their families—and the quality—the real attention they were able to give them. The authors noted the "feeling that work drains so much energy that there is little left to invest actively in family pursuits." They comment:

> Home has become a place for recuperation in a supportive atmosphere—an impoverished way of thinking of private life.

Even though he is dissatisfied, the manager is unlikely to change, to turn more of his time and energy toward home. He feels he can't, and if you dig deeper he begins to realize he doesn't really want to. At first he complains about the demands and pressures, but a few minutes later he is confiding that he likes the pressures; he wants to be where the action is; fulfilling the demands is fulfilling to himself. In other words, his need for achievement must be met, even at the expense of his need for emotional support and love. The authors say:

And here, in a nutshell, is his paradox. He does *not* want to make choices. He wants the best of both worlds —the best of professional life and the best of private life.

Both the man's own nature and his wife's attitude make a major difference to his sense of satisfaction with his lifestyle. Another important factor is the culture of the organization for which he works. Equally effective companies can work in dramatically different ways, with equally different effects on the home lives of their managers. I know one company that makes extraordinary demands on the time of its members, expecting them to "do their homework" on every conceivable thing that might go wrong and treating quite mundane matters as crises deserving of weekend-long meetings. At the same time, the culture demands (and gets) people who are able to maintain solid home lives; I think they select the kinds of young people who are likely to marry the kinds of people who can cope with the time demands and share the sense of membership that goes with it. In another company (and most Japanese companies), the manager is frowned upon if he isn't seen to be leaving and arriving at the same time as his people—not later and not earlier.

The wives, too, are often ambivalent, feeling they must choose between family life and their outside interests and at the same time trying to live up to their own assumptions about the right way for the wife of a manager to behave, which are often at odds with their personal needs for attention and emotional support.

Then, too, you have the manager's personality. The research showed that the so-called Type A person—the impulsive, competitive perfectionist—is not only likely to suffer more heart attacks or other stress-related illness, but also is much more likely to feel dissatisfied with his life-style (and perhaps less likely to do anything to balance it?).

One of the most important aspects in achieving balance

between home and working lives is the age of the manager. Bartolomé and Evans refer to "life stages"; Gail Sheehy subtitled her book "Predictable Crises of Adult Life." Put very simply, our needs, interests, and abilities grow at different paces on different fronts.

One of the things I learned early (probably from Dr. Spock) in my child-rearing days was the funny stop-go pattern of development as a child grew. One week your toddler is vividly physical, trying out new muscles and skills, barging into things, hitting you, generally moving all the time. Another week and he's growing emotionally, exploring new feelings, expressing a need for cuddling, or acting out his pains as if he were Theda Bara. And a week later he's learning new words, asking "why" constantly, putting together ideas from different people and generally behaving as a three-year-old intellectual. As he gets older the phases last a bit longer, and you see them dovetailing into each other. Perhaps these intellectual, emotional, and physical phases of growth are like biorhythms in that they work on different time scales, so it's possible to be low on all three or high on all three, but most of the time one or another is demonstrably ahead or behind.

These are natural cycles, certainly, and Sheehy points out that they extend into adult life in some ways, but their manifestations are different for women and men, and thus husbands and wives can get "out of phase" with each other, even though their basic values and life-style are well matched.

Bartolomé and Evans describe these imbalances as they affect managers in particular. The early years, into the early thirties certainly, might be called the "launching" phase. The young manager is increasingly focused on his career, in a "spiral of success," and the family is likely to take a significantly secondary place in his priorities. His wife at this stage may be dissatisfied with the amount and quality of time and attention she and the family get, but he is not apt to pay much heed to her demands. If he changes the balance in his life-style at this stage, it is more often because of the children rather than because of his wife.

As mid-life approaches—somewhere in the range from the late thirties to the mid-forties—the manager is usually turning his attention toward his private life. If the balance between the two is mentioned in a gathering of managers in this stage, it often raises the emotional temperature, because this is a fundamental issue to many of them. But at the same time, his wife at this stage is likely to be giving up her attempts to get more attention, and instead looking for outside interests to fill the emotional or intellectual void. If the couple are lucky (or wise—or still in touch with each other) there is a chance to connect, to rewrite the marriage contract, before they pass each other like ships in the dark, each sending semaphore messages the other doesn't see.

The demands of the children are likely to be changing, too, as they go into their teens and begin challenging parental authority, testing limits, trying out new values and attitudes. At the same time, they are more likely to be able to share interests with their father and take part in mutually satisfying activities. One thirty-eight-year-old manager said: "In ten years the children will be off my hands altogether, and the amount of time that I've spent with them—although there have been good moments—has *certainly* been too little."

In the late thirties and early forties, the researchers found five different ways that people coped with the stresses:

* *Confirmation.* This manager has made a success of his career at work, his career as a husband, and his career as a father, even though the work has probably taken precedence. At this stage he may feel a sense of being confirmed in his approaches and attitudes. However, this may be an illusion, especially if it is upset by changes in the interests of his wife and offspring.

* *Renegotiation.* The manager has made a success at work and turns his anxieties to the home front, "sparking off an often painful period of renegotiation of the marriage and life-style." This pain may be a prerequisite to better individual development for both partners later, as well as their partnership improving.

* *Status Quo.* The managers who felt tense and dissatisfied with their marriages were often afraid to "unleash the storm of marital renegotiation," because their marriages were nonetheless increasing in importance to them. The result is likely to be petty bickering, which gives an outlet for tensions of both partners. Underneath it all, he's probably unwilling to change his career orientation, so this approach continues with self-justification and attempts to get his wife to adapt better to the life-style he chooses. This approach tends to be favored by people whose careers have been only partly successful.

* *Turning Point.* The manager who didn't find a career to fit his abilities in the launching phase may compensate as mid-life approaches by looking for much more of his satisfaction in the family relationships. He actually changes the balance of time he invests in each and tends to think about "work" rather than "career," while he focuses much more attention on his family.

* *Late Success.* Some people, particularly those who spent the "launching" years in technical careers and thus spent much more attention on their families, discover around mid-life that they get much more satisfaction at work as management assignments increase. The man feels turned on at work for the first time in his life, and of course he invests his time

/ 249

accordingly. He is the one who feels the cost in family involvement most sharply, because he tended to have more family contact in the earlier years.

This is the life stage where the manager resolves the balance; the older managers don't like talking about the balance much, either because it was satisfying, or because it wasn't; in either case, the resolution is past history. The researchers found two distinctly different patterns among the older managers.

Those who had not resolved the private/professional aspects of their lives simply went on in a "maintenance" mode, learning to live with the fragmented life-style, increasingly resigned to things as they are. They are probably not happy about the status of the marriage, but they've gone beyond worrying about it, and the wife has developed her own interests as the children have grown up. They regard themselves as a little dull, and that seems to be the flavor of their lives, too. They feel (usually correctly) that they have topped out at work; they are earning well, but the achievements are no longer as satisfying, or as frequent. Any bitterness is likely to shift toward a fatalistic shrug and decreasing interest in most aspects of life. The authors note one exception:

> One preoccupation may grow—the concern for his relationship with his adolescent children; this probably is colored with a belated hope of helping them to realize themselves in a way in which he was unable to develop himself.

The other path for the older manager is called "generativity." This is the win/win game, in which the manager becomes a mentor or sponsor, gaining some of his own satisfactions from the achievements of those he is helping in their own development—and those people may include his wife and maturing offspring. This path is marked by "a renewed internal sense of purpose and of confidence, a renewed self and fresh enthusiasm." He goes about his old tasks in new ways, or he looks for new tasks and avocations. This is the older manager who has looked at the yin and yang and found ways to fuse them. He wants and gets both the achievement and success that work can offer and the emotional closeness that can come at home. He is more likely to view his organization as a "family" to which he's responsible and to view his home life as a "career" that demands care and management.

This is the man who goes to the top, the one who breaks the stereotype. As his enthusiasm increases, he shifts his attention from individual achievements to relationships with others, and he is therefore able to achieve more through their efforts. His own increasing assurance is one more factor that can help assure his progress into the most senior ranks of management.

Chapter 27.

IDENTITIES AND DESTINATIONS

Managers, like employees in general, are likely to be a good deal more "fireproof" in the future, either by law or custom. If a manager becomes a lifetime resource for a company, then the company and the manager both need to recognize the various stages of growth and their implications. If the manager can pass through the different stages of his career with maximum opportunities to learn, to feel positive and enthusiastic, and to integrate the various aspects of his life, both he and the company are winners.

No Mid-Life Crisis!

In the last chapter I avoided using two overpopular terms about the middle stage. The first is "mid-life crisis"; the second is "male menopause." Both are nonsense!

Every one of us has to go through the forty mark at some point, and many of us find reasons in our lives to re-evaluate our attitudes around that time. This is not a "crisis" but a natural phenomenon and one we can learn to accept more gracefully, or even welcome. As to the menopause image, it's not only silly but also harmful, because it can induce a fear of the process with overtones of waning masculinity. The correlation, if one must be made, is much more appropriate if one compares it to the re-evaluation a woman goes through when her children first get into school. Her priorities must change if she is to go on, beyond the pre-programmed Madonna images, or the shiny-floors/shiny-hair pictures on the television screen, to some new life-style that will be satisfying for the rest of her life.

I tended to call this the "forty-one phenomenon" because I saw three different managers change their styles quite radically on or around their forty-first birthdays a few years ago. Today I think we have to settle for "mid-life," because it is clear that younger managers are re-examining their values, too, perhaps because values are changing quite rapidly in society as a whole. The phenomenon may be most severe in people who have grown up with a fairly explicit "program" (in the sense of a computer program) or picture of what their lives and roles will be like and then reach a point where they must depart from the program or scenario into less-charted realms. This is particularly true of the people who were children in the prewar years and became adults just after the war. The more stable world of smaller towns and smaller firms and eternal values evaporated into urban living, high technology, big business, nuclear families, and instant neighborhoods. Most of us coped, often quite well, but underneath it all we were still fettered with those old pictures of who we were and how we behaved and what we expected from life. I think our children may be more adept at doing their re-evaluating in manageable bites, rather than trying to gulp it all down at one sitting.

As Gail Sheehy points out in *Passages* and Warren Bennis noted in the mid-sixties, mid-life is not the only peak in such questioning. In fact, a rich life probably has quite a few such points of introspection. Sheehy describes the period, perhaps in the eighteen to twenty-three region, when young people will go to considerable lengths to defer the who-am-I? or "identity" question. It tends to resolve itself somewhere in the twenty-three to twenty-seven range.

I was looking at the management leakage tables for an IBM company and this showed up quite sharply. Young people came in after graduation, and quite a number of them left in the year or so around twenty-five. They were saying to themselves, in essence: "I am not an IBMer." From the company's viewpoint, this may be a nuisance, but other recruits are usually not difficult to find. The other bump on the chart presented a different problem, though. This occurred in the three years either side of forty—a wider but lower bump. However, those managers, responding to the where-am-I-going? or "destination" question, represented a great loss in know-how, as well as linkage in the organization.

One wife put it in a nutshell on the morning of her husband's fortieth birthday. "Honey," she said, "I suspect in the next year you're either going to buy a boat or take a mistress or change your job. Let's go boat-shopping." (He actually changed his job seven months later.) This is the stage in which people sometimes make quite drastic changes in their life-styles. Hair styles change; new clothes are bought to depict new self-images; new hobbies and interests are often pursued with frightening intensity. Often these changes around the fringes or on the surface of a man's life are attempts to keep the phenomenon under control, to manage it, to keep the deeper implications at bay.

I worry most about the people who sail serenely through the early forties without a change of any sort, without confronting the old program and trying to develop a workable new one for the rest of their lives. The destination question afflicts all of us, and most of our programs really *do* run out somewhere in the early forties. Women are brought up for wifing and mothering, especially the latter, and children emerging from their teens don't want much more mothering. The old Horatio Alger pattern infuses the programs of most men: onward and upward. Somewhere around forty it usually becomes clear that the "upward" has its limits—and it may not even be a path that is attractive any more, much less attainable. We look over our shoulders and see packs of young tigers nipping at our heels. We look at those around us who are in their fifties and sixties, who have settled back into "maintenance" modes and subsided into organizational backwaters. We have twenty or twenty-five years to go in our working lives. How are we going to spend them? It's a serious question, and it *does* merit a year or two of contemplation.

But it's not all an intellectual, logical, yang process. There's a yin element, too. No matter how much you know about mid-life re-evaluation, no matter how wise your family or firm, when it happens, it can be devastating! One's first reaction is often depression. You have to get through this, and consciously seek out alternatives and look at them, before you can gather the emotional resources to rewrite that program, to tell yourself and your confreres who you are and who you intend to be for the rest of your life. The progam doesn't rewrite itself overnight. The review of old values can't quite be planned. The new patterns emerge gradually, during the course of a year or five years—or even ten. The important thing is to let it happen, to seek out new possibilities, and to retain some kind of feeling that you "own" yourself, as well as the process you are going through. This means renegotiating contracts not just with your wife or children or company, but renegotiating contracts with yourself.

Twenty-Five Years More of This?

Mid-life demands intellectual and emotional energy. There is also a physical element. (This is where the "male menopause" image can be so harmful.) We are getting a little more creaky; gray hair shows up, or hairlines recede. Images of youthful vigor seem to crop up accusingly on all sides. We worry about waning sexual interest—which helps explain a good many mid-life divorces, I think, along with a "twenty-five years or more!" picture analogous to the working imagery. Bartolomé and Lee Evans studied a population of married managers, but the number who are divorced at mid-life is increasing. I once visited a lively singles apartment complex in California on a Friday night. Most of the men seemed to be within a couple of years of forty. Most of the women were in their late twenties; my friend in her early thirties was one of the oldest women living there. On the surface it was a picture worthy of *Playboy*, with trendy clothes, trendy music, plenty of action. But if you listened to the undercurrents, it was slightly sad. Most of the "liberated" women were doing cooking, washing, and so on for the "liberated" men, hoping rather wistfully that husbands of their own might be found through this process. And most of the men seemed to be waiting for the next day when they could visit their children or worrying about the cost of maintaining two households or jumping whenever the phone rang, because it might herald a break in the cold war with the estranged spouse. A slightly ritualistic "no commitments" flavor lurked under the physical freedom.

The manager who undergoes a mid-life divorce is naturally thrown back onto his career for most of his emotional fulfillment, as well as his achievements. But this occurs just as he is most likely to be turning the focus *away* from work, and any re-evaluation may be hampered as a result. Some second marriages occur at this point (thereby creating a natural focus for new emotional patterns at home and avoiding the painful renegotiation phase the married colleagues have to traverse), but people emerging from a failed marriage are likely to be cautious, as well as impecunious, as well as guilt-ridden—an inauspicious start. Divorce can certainly be a catalyst for the whole process of renegotiating contracts with yourself, but I think the process usually takes longer under these circumstances, and you have to do it without the comfortable home environment you can take for granted as a backdrop.

Henry VIII was married to Catherine of Aragon for nearly twenty years. At thirty-eight he upset the applecart (and the world) and embarked on a different marital career. His other five wives were acquired during the next nine years.

Gail Sheehy describes research with a group of junior (thirties) and senior (average age fifty-three) analysts:

> The senior therapists are less likely to blame the marital partner for problems; whereas the junior therapists believe they can assign blame to one partner or the other and do *not* see marriage as a process that follows different stages. For the older people the terrific competitiveness with the other, all others, has relaxed, and more personalized enjoyments can be sought. As distinct from their juniors, they stress that the middle years are a release from pressures of involvement. The greatest freedom of all has opened up; the freedom to be independent and self-sufficient within any relationship.

These are the people who could be most valuable, not only to themselves and their families, but also to their companies. The company has little say in how gracefully an individual manager goes through mid-life, though it might do more throughout his career to give him time and opportunities to look at his values and his career in more manageable bites. Ultimately, the company's vitality depends on its ability to get and retain (through mid-life years and beyond) good managers, so the joint investment in an individual's development makes sense. An organization that contains a healthy population of these serene seniors, whose well-integrated lives can create potential patterns for others, has a better chance of maintaining balance, not only in ages but also in attitudes.

One thing an organization could do at this point (or any other!) is make it easier for people who have redefined their destinations, or are trying to do so, to try out new activities, even new careers, within the organization. If "appraisal" and "assessment" are carried out with the individual's own needs and interests as the focus (as they already are in a few leading companies), then a touch of staleness or dissatisfaction can be voiced, discussed, and used as a basis for development, even in radically different directions. The technical man who discovers a glimmer of personnel interest could spend a stint as a gatekeeper or butterfly between the two areas. The dissatisfied general manager could think about directions for a sabbatical leave and go out and research a problem that concerns him.

I know one executive in his fifties whose company gave him a three-month leave of absence and a little cash (so he could take his wife) to go to several foreign countries and study how pre-retirement managers were being handled in various firms. He is adamant, incidentally, that "retirement age" should be a personal decision, rather than a matter of company policy. Some people want to leave as soon as possible—especially those who have been marking time, with their focus outside the company. Some would like to leave while they have the energy (and some pension assistance) to start new and vastly different careers. These people probably help the company by going early, because they make space for other managers to enjoy continued development. (The crystals from which transistors are made are notable as much for their holes, into and out of which electrons pop like marbles, as for the material around the holes.)

Then there are the managers who live for their work, and the law that lets them work until they're seventy is probably a lifesaver—literally. The company of the future—and a good many current companies—will make room for retirement, like development, to be a personal decision as much as possible. It may also help, for those who are retiring in the foreseeable future, to offer a selection of courses, on company time, covering not only the legal and health aspects that many preretirement courses include, but also such practical things as how to maintain your own car or do-it-yourself skills or other activities suited to managers who suddenly find they have more time and a bit less money.

Finally, it would make sense to raise the question of

whether companies, like the individuals within them, go through these phases, resolving questions of identity and destination. I can think of a number I have seen weather the identity phase. It is more likely that the destination phase is usually put off by a company. And just like an individual, the company that does so is consigning itself to a less fruitful and integrated future. If ways can be found to bring the question to the surface and at least nibble around its edges, the company has a better chance to avoid the freezing and bureaucracy that characterize well-maintained but fragmented lives.

Chapter 28.

FULL CIRCLE

Fifteen years ago a mathematical friend taught me about Möbius strips and Fibinacci series. A Möbius strip is simply a strip of paper to which you give a single half-twist and then Scotch-tape the ends together. It has intriguing properties: if you start to color it with a red pen on one side and a blue pen on the other, you find the red running into the blue and vice versa. If you cut it in half, you get a single circle, only twice as long. If you cut it in thirds, you get a long one and a short one. The ramifications are fun, and my office was festooned with colored, complicated cut-up Möbius strips. But while I was doodling these, I was also trying to figure out how the opposite sides of a piece of paper could become the same side. I've been trying to do the same thing with ideas, with people, with organizations, ever since. Where is the half-twist?

Another beautiful pattern is the double helix, the shape of the basic elements that determine human characteristics, the DNA inside the human cell. The double helix implies motion, roundness, natural cycles—the breath, the tides, the sunrises, or the electromagnetic vibrations from one pole to another, that give us color and sound and X-rays and ultraviolet and television ads. Because these natural changes in frequency and amplitude also carry information. We have learned to harness some of them and use them for our own purposes, to impose our own patterns on them. It seems to me that natural human rhythms also merit such respect; as we learn more about them we can use these, too, to carry information, or impart color in our individual and group and organizational lives.

It was the ideas of yin and yang that brought me full circle, back to the Möbius strip and the Fibinacci series. Because the beautiful Fibinacci pattern, which comes out of a quadratic equation and the progress of logarithms, is expressed in nature by the whorls of a seashell. You can find it in a photograph of a grand circular staircase ascending a few floors. In life I like the picture of a person's development as a series of ever-widening spirals, each perhaps made up of chambers, like the shell of the crustacean. Astronomers tell us this is the shape of the universe. This is the logarithmic spiral. It is the shape of the foetus. And in the realm of ideas, it was startling to find that the yin and yang symbols are actually made up from such spirals.

From the sublime to the ridiculous, from the universe to the human cell, from the feelings to the concepts, from yin to yang, we must constantly name things and order them, in order to cope with the variety in our world.

Managers are no exception. Every month some management magazine comes up with new categories, new names, new descriptions, new "roles." I've coined a few myself herein, because a book, like the left hemisphere of the brain, is a sequential thing, and categories help keep information under control. Some useful categories have popped up in the course of the years. Before the manager-naming tendency reached fad proportions, *Fortune* noted the "thinker" and the "doer." Antony Jay talked about the "yogi" and the "commissar." Michael Maccoby has "gamesmen" and "craftsmen."

These can often help us if they give us a picture of new possibilities. On the other hand, they can be limiting if they superimpose someone else's pictures on our own patterns, and we have to lop off those bits that don't quite fit. The half-twist is learning how to use categories—*especially* categories of managers—to give us new space, without squeezing or cutting our own selves and our realms of interest and activity.

Clark Dorsey, a duPont executive, was talking about a couple of his favorite categories (the "German dictator" and the "gee-whiz manager" among others) when he said: "The best managers seem able to shift whenever it's suitable." They can tailor their performance to the expectations of their superiors (and nowadays their peers and subordinates), or they can switch to another organization that fits them better. "We don't have many German dictator-type managers around these days. German dictators have gone out of fashion."

Ah, but we still need a bit of autocracy now and then, someone to project a bit of authority when we feel somewhat lost. And we still need scientific management, with all its implications, at least in some measure. We need that hard-headed left hemisphere just as much as the instinctive right one I've spent so much space on herein. That is the message of yin and yang, that they are two portions of a completeness.

We are heading into an era in which human aspects of management are likely to take precedence over technical aspects. This is perhaps overdue, but (being human) we will probably overdo it. That kind of swinging from pole to pole is also inherent in the yin and yang. There is energy in such oscillation, and we should learn to harness it.

Balance is difficult, the delicate position between the "on" and "off" marks of the switch, the point where biorhythms go critical, the transition from one state to another. Perfect balance, in a living system as in an organization, is neither possible nor desirable, but a sense of aspiring toward balance could be helpful, and a sense of the wholeness of the organization, with respect for its less logical aspects, can also help keep its elements youthful, or at least renewing themselves.

It is the nature of living systems to try to replicate themselves—a sense of survival of the species lies under the reproductive drive. It is also the nature of living systems ultimately to die. From a certain age (quite alarmingly, in one's twenties) the cells of the body are dying slightly faster than we are replacing them. Eventually, the process gets more imbalanced and one organism dies. If we take better care of it, it will probably serve us a little longer or better. Similarly, an organization or group that is properly nourished, with a healthy chemical balance and a zestful outlook, one whose elements are free to develop and learn, will serve us a little longer or better, too.

Human ideas are handed on from one generation to another, amended to fit new circumstances, and fleshed out with new examples. Some come into fashion and then fade in another kind of natural cycle. We are beginning to realize that organizations, too, hand on their cultures, their concepts, and their "genetic material" long after the original living system is gone. If today's managers can use the useful messages from previous organizations and adapt them to the world ahead, I am quite hopeful for the future of management.

BIBLIOGRAPHY

Bailey, F. G., *Stratagems and Spoils: A Social Anthropology of Politics,* Basil Blackwell, Oxford, 1969.

Bannister, D., and Fay Fransella, *Inquiring Man: The Theory of Personal Constructs,* Penguin, London, 1971.

Bartolomé, Fernando, and Paul A. Lee Evans, "Professional Lives Versus Private Lives—Shifting Patterns of Management Commitment," *Organizational Dynamics,* AMA, spring 1979.

Belbin, R. M., B. R. Aston, and R. D. Mottram, "Building Effective Management Teams," *Journal of General Management,* Vol. 3, No. 3, spring 1976.

Bennis, Warren, *Organization Development: Its Nature, Origins and Prospects,* Addison-Wesley, Reading, Mass., 1969.

Bennis, Warren, and Philip Slater, *The Temporary Society,* Harper & Row, New York, 1968.

Berg, Per-Olof, *Emotional Structures in Organizations: A Study of the Process of Change in a Swedish Company,* Studentlitteratur, Lund (Sweden), 1979.

Berry, Dean F., "Gardens and Graveyards in Management Education," *Management Education,* OECD (Paris), 1972.

Boettinger, Henry, "Some Aspects of Politics and Power in Our Time," in *The Individual, the Enterprise and the State* (ed. R. I. Tricker), Associated Business Programmes, London, 1977.

Boxer, Philip J. *Developing the Quality of Judgment,* London Business School, May 1977.

Braun, Ernest, "Homo Faber, Homo Ludens and the Future of Work," in *Science and Technology and the Future* (eds. H. Buchholz and W. Grielin), K. G. Saur, Munich, 1979.

Burgoyne, John, Tom Boydell, and Mike Pedler, *Self Development: Theory and Applications for Practitioners*, Association of Teachers of Management, London, 1978.

Casey, David, and David Pearce, *More Than Management Development*, Gower Press, London, 1977. (Available through AMA in US.)

Collins, Eliza G. C., "Everyone who makes it has a mentor," *Harvard Business Review*, July–August 1978.

Cooper, Cary, and Barbara Lewis, "The Femanager Boom," *Management Today* (London), July 1979.

Cunningham, Ian, *Self-Managed Learning*, Anglian Regional Management Centre (Chelmsford, Essex), June 1978.

Domhoff, G. William, "But Why Did They Sit on the King's Right in the First Place?", *Psychoanalytic Review*, 56 (1969–70).

Foy, Nancy, *The Sun Never Sets on IBM*, Morrow, New York, 1975.

———, "Worker Participation: Contrasts in Three Countries," *Harvard Business Review*, May–June 1976.

———, "Action Learning Comes to Industry," *Harvard Business Review*, September–October 1977.

Gellerman, Saul W., "Developing Managers Without Management Development," *The Conference Board Record*, July 1973.

Grayson, C. J., "Management Science and Business Practice," *Harvard Business Review*, July–August 1973.

Gyllenhammar, Pehr, *People at Work*, Addison-Wesley, Reading, Mass., 1977.

Handy, Charles, "Pitfalls of Management Development," *Personnel Management* (London), February 1974.

———, *Gods of Management*, Souvenir Press (London), 1978.

Hansen, Harry L., *British Managers in the Mirror*, Advanced Management Programmes International (London), 1974.

Harrison, Roger, "How to Describe Your Organization," *Harvard Business Review*, May–June 1972.

Hedberg, Bo L. T., Paul C. Nystrom, and William H. Starbuck,

"Camping on Seesaws: Prescriptions for a Self-Designing Organization," *Administrative Science Quarterly*, March 1976.

Jay, Antony, *Management and Machiavelli*, Hodder & Stoughton, London, 1967.

———, "Nobody's Perfect—but a team can be," *Observer Magazine* (London), 20 April 1980.

———, *Corporation Man*, Jonathan Cape (London), 1972.

Kaje, Ritva, "Bringing the Feminine into Forecasting: Foreseeing and Learning," in *Futures Research: New Directions* (eds. Harold A. Linstone and W. H. Clive Simmonds), Addison-Wesley, Reading, Mass., 1977.

Koestler, Arthur, *Janus: A Summing Up*, Hutchinson, London, 1978.

Kolb, David A., and Richard E. Boyatzis, "On the Dynamics of the Helping Relationship," *Journal of Applied Behavioral Science*, Vol. 6, No. 3, 1970.

Maccoby, Michael, *The Gamesmen, the New Corporate Leaders*, Simon & Schuster, New York, 1977.

Mant, Alistair, *The Rise and Fall of the British Manager*, Macmillan, London, 1977.

March, James G., "The Technology of Foolishness," in *Ambiguity and Choice in Organizations* (ed. James G. March and Johan P. Olsen), Universitetsforlaget (Oslo), 1976.

Miller, James G., "Living Systems: Basic Concepts," *Behavioral Science*, Vol. 10, No. 3, July 1965.

Mintzberg, Henry, *The Nature of Managerial Work*, Harper & Row, New York, 1973.

Morris, John, "Developing Resourceful Managers," in *Management Development and Training Handbook* (eds. B. Taylor & G. L. Lippitt), McGraw-Hill, New York, 1975.

MacRae, Norman, "The Coming Entrepreneurial Revolution," *The Economist* (London), 25 December 1976.

McClelland, David C., *The Achieving Society*, Van Nostrand, New York, 1961.

McFadden, Cyra, *The Serial: A Year in the Life of Marin County*, Knopf, New York, 1977.

Nadelson, Theodore, and Leon Eisenberg, "The Successful Professional Woman: On Being Married to One," *American Journal of Psychiatry*, October 1977.

Nind, Philip, "Education for Corporate Responsibility," in *Productivity and Amenity—Achieving a Social Balance*, Croon & Helm (London), 1973.

Ornstein, Robert E., *The Psychology of Consciousness*, W. H. Freeman, London, 1972.

Pascale, Richard Tanner, "Zen and the Art of Management," *Harvard Business Review*, March–April 1978 (1978 McKinsey Award winner).

Peter, L. J., and Raymond Hull, *The Peter Principle*, Morrow, New York, 1969.

Pettigrew, Andrew M., *The Politics of Organizational Decision-Making*, Tavistock (London), 1973.

——, "Towards a Political Theory of Organizational Intervention," *Human Relations*, Vol. 28, No. 3, 1975.

Pfeiffer, J. W., and J. E. Jones (eds.), *Annual Handbooks for Group Facilitators*, University Associates (Calif.), 1972–78.

Pocock Committee, *Educational and Training Needs of European Managers*, European Foundation for Management Development (Brussels), 1977.

Potter, Stephen, *Complete Upmanship*, Holt, Rinehart & Winston, New York, 1971.

Rapoport, R. N., *Mid-Career Development*, Tavistock (London), 1970.

Rapoport, Robert and Rhona, *Dual Career Families*, Penguin, London, 1971.

Revans, R. W., "Management Education: time for a rethink," *Personnel Management* (London), July 1976.

Sheane, Derek, "Organisation Development in Action," *Journal of European Training*, Vol. 2, No. 8, 1978.

Sheehy, Gail, *Passages*, Dutton, New York, 1974.

Shein, Edgar, *Career Dynamics*, Addison-Wesley, Reading, Mass., 1978.

Smith, Hedrick, *Russians*, Ballantine, New York, 1977.

Stewart, Rosemary, *Contrasts in Management,* McGraw-Hill, New York, 1976.

Stiskin, Nahum, *The Looking-Glass God: Shinto, Yin-Yang, and a Cosmology for Today,* Autumn Press, Brookline, Mass., 1972.

Tricker, R. I., "Order or Freedom—The Ultimate Issue in Information Systems Design," IAG Workshop, Denmark, 1978.

Weinstein, Bill, "Political Education for Management: Luxury or Necessity?" Working Paper, Balliol College (Oxford), 1975.

INDEX

Change agents (cont.)
needed by, 192–197; blocked by
managers, 187; composite characteristics of,. 188–189; creation of other
change agents by, 193–197; and
crisis, 185; defined, 190; and holdouts, 184; personality characteristics
essential for, 191–192; potential, see
Potential change agents; roles of,
192; as systems analysts, 202; titles
for, 189–190
Changes: and consultants, 211–215; in
mid-life, 252–253. See also Change
agents; Organizational change
Child-rearing, by career women,
44–45
Children of managers, attitudes
toward organizations, 55–57
Closed question, 206–207
Coalitions, building of, 197, 203
Cochrane, Richard, 199
"Cock-up theory of history," 59
"Co-consulting," 137–138, 235–236
Communications: careers for women
in, 47–48; in computer industry,
73–74; of consultant's finding, 211–
213; importance of, 113
"Community support" campaigns,
companies involved in, 158
Company paper, speak-up column in,
103
Complaints. See Letters of complaint
Computer industry: communication
problem in, 73–74; mergers in, 158–
159; project teams in, 131–132
Conceptualizer. See Outsider
Confidence, in autonomous groups,
141
Confirmation, in mid-life, 248
Conflict, use by consultants, 215
Conglomerates. See Acquisitions and
mergers
Consciousness-raising, 196, 197
"Conspiracy theory of history," 59
Consultancy skills, and co-consulting,
138
Consultant(s): arrangements with,
213–214; characteristics necessary
for, 202; "innocent" model of, 201;
as scapegoat, 216. See also Do-it-
yourself consultants
Consumerism, 20, 161
Contact man, 145–149
Contracts: with consultant, 213; in
management education, 242; rene-
gotiating in mid-life, 255
Convention, for network, 121–122
Corporate culture(s), 150–160; and acquisitions and mergers, 158–160;

attitudes toward home lives and,
246; difficulties of analysis of, 153–
155; foreign, action learning and,
220; and hiring policy, 156–158;
impact of past history on, 154–156;
Japanese and American companies
compared, 152; manifestations of,
150–152; and project teams, 135–
136; and relationships between
companies, 158; seen from outside,
157–158
Corporate policies, changing from
outside. See Managing from outside
Corporate sociologists, creation of,
160
Corporation history, impact on
present, 154–156
Corsey, Clark, 262
Courses: for do-it-yourself consultants, 201–202; for potential change
agents, 199–200. See also Management education
Creativity, 62–66; of butterfly, 128–
129; and doubters, 105; encouragement of, 66–69; and freedom and
order, 69–70; and group work, 168;
and models, 74; and moonlight
projects and bootlegged innovations, 169–171; and networks, 117
Credibility: and change agentry, 197;
of leader, 77; of "management information," 113
Crisis, and achievement of critical
mass, 184–185
Crisis management, 23
Critic, 146
Critical element, and management, 38
Critical mass: in advertising, 182; creation of, 182–185; clustering and,
185–186; and management education, 185–186; in physics, 181–182
Criticism: and "brainstorming," 68;
in interviews, 208, 209
"Crown-prince syndrome," 233–234
Cultural conditioning, and intuitive
capacity, 37
Culture, and yin and yang elements
of management, 38–39

Data collection and analysis, of
consultants, 214
Decentralization, and increased
outside demands, 19
Decision-making: and creativity, 67;
and participative leadership, 84;
productivity and, 178–179; workers
and, 24–25
Delegation, 93

Group thinking, influence on individuals, 182
Groups of networks, 121

Halford, Ron, 96, 199
Harvard Business School, leadership development and, 83–84
Headquarters for network, 122
Heller, Walter, 19
Hiring policy: and corporate culture, 156–158; and locating change agents, 198–199; in self-sustaining organizations, 174; and young MBAs, 231–232
Holdouts, reinforcement of trends and, 184
Holte, Johan, 81
Home, role of. See Family relationships
Homo ludens, 53–54
Honesty, in interviews, 208
Honeywell, 157, 159
Hsi, Fu, 32
Human biorhythms, work schedules and, 38
Human rights demands, in future, 20
Hurst, Marjorie, 46–47
Hypocrisy, attitude toward, 67

IBM, 102; domestic and world trade, 85–86; hiring policies, 156–157; informal information in, 113–114; "Open Door" policy, 164–166; sense of membership in, 103–104
Idea, planting in group, 183–184
Ideas Man, 143, 145–146, 183; and self-sustaining organizations, 168–169
Images: in mid-life, 252–253; persistence of, 109–110; and women as spiders, 126
"Implementers," 146; innovators and, 177
Individual growth, compared to group growth, 139
Individual innovation, group ownership and, 167–169
Inflation, 20, 22
Informal information, 113–115; training program on, 129–130. See also Informal networks; Networks
Informal networks: size of, 115; and flow of informal information, 115–116; law of effectiveness and, 117–118; and managing upwards, 123–124; and trust, 116; uses for, 116–117; as windows in internal walls, 88

Informal reward system, ongoing achievement and, 168
Informality, boundary crossing and, 98
Information: and autonomous groups, 141; games that deal with, 58
Information explosion, suppression of creativity and, 65–66
Information flow: managing upwards and, 123; network building and, 119
"Information overload," 63, 98
"Information science," 113
Innovations, 176–177; bootlegged, 169–171; shared ownership in, 174; transferability of, 167–169
INSEAD, 244
Inside catalysts, as change agents, 192
Insider/outsider coalitions, 197
Inspector, 147
"Inspectors," 147; innovators and, 177
Inspiration, and creativity, 62
Internal walls, compared with boundaries, 91; and re-entry problems, 89–90; windows in, 87–88
International companies, in future, 20–23
Interrupting, in interviews, 209
"Interviewing skills," 206–209
Intuitiveness: attitudes toward, 66–67; of change agent, 189; of managers, 36–38

Japanese companies, 38–39; social and recreational employee facilities of, 152
Jargon, in interviews, 209
Job enlargement, 93–95
Job security, 25
Jobs, in future, 21. See also Work
"Joint Development Activity" ("JDA"), 220
Joint ventures, 22
Journalists, networks and, 116–117
Jucraft, Frank, 92

Kendall, Sir Maurice, 62
Kennedy, John F., 83
"Key actors," corporate culture and, 154
"Key informants," corporate culture and, 154

Language, of different organizational levels, 196
Language skills, change agentry and, 196
Lao-tzu, 174

Visibility, and beginning managers, 233–234
Vocations, of potential change agents, 199
Voluntariness, and managing upwards, 123
Volvo, Sweden, 81, 140, 142–143
Von Boeschoten, Marjo, 228

Walls: informal networks and, 115–116; and ownership and membership, 101
Watson, James, 117
Watson, Thomas J., 86
Windows, 88; created by informal networks, 115; projects as, 132
Win/lose games: cost of, 57–58; status games as, 60–61
Winning, as fun, 54–55
Win/win games, 57–58, 123; project teams as, 135; and world outlook, 58–59
Wives of managers. *See* Family relationships
Women: details and, 41, 43; equal opportunities for, 44–46; and increasing yin nature of organizations, 49–51; intuitive qualities of, 36–38, 40–44; nonstandard career approaches for, 45–49; opportunities for, 49; in organizations, 40–51; as spiders, 126–127; and success, 44–50
Women's liberation movement, 43
Word-of-mouth, and change, 184
Work: changed attitudes of young people toward, 52; changes in, 30; and creativity, 62

Worker participation, productivity and, 178–179
Work ethic, shift to leisure ethic, 179–180
Work force size, in future, 21
Working group. *See* Autonomous groups
Working hours, flexible, 30
World outlook, and win/win games, 58–59

Yang. *See* Yin and Yang
Yin. *See* Yin and Yang
Yin and Yang, 32–39; and brain hemispheres, 34–35; and business schools, 222; interplay of, 35; of learning, 237, 241; and management, 36–37; and management development and education, 217; and management distinguished from leadership, 75–76; and men and women in organizations, 40–51; in mid-life, 251, 255; and Möbius strip and the Fibinacci series, 261; and organizational change, 175, 262–263; philosophy of, 33–34

Young managers: and balance in lifestyle, 247–248; training of, 231–236
Young people: changed attitudes toward work, 52; and management jobs, 26. *See also* MBAs

"Zero-sum games," 58
Zest factor. *See* Fun

THE AUTHOR

Nancy Foy became an internationally known management expert through a series of largely intuitive leaps into the unknown —from suburban wife and mother into the heyday of the aerospace and computer industries in California, then into international journalism in London, into shop-floor participation in Sweden, into management research at Oxford, into management in London. This diversity of experience has reinforced her view that organizations are living entities with personalities or "cultures" as unique as those of individuals.

She is best known for her 1975 book, *The Sun Never Sets on IBM*, a study of the company's international customs, culture, and behavior. She also wrote *Computer Management: A Common-Sense Approach*, co-authored *Presidential Leadership and University Change* (with Warren Bennis), and collaborated with Pehr Gyllenhammar in writing *People at Work*. Among her many articles is the landmark study of shop-floor participation in Sweden, Britain, and the United States, published in the *Harvard Business Review* in 1977 and currently used in companies and business schools in many countries.

Nancy is currently a manager in Standard Telephones and Cables Ltd., the UK subsidiary of ITT. When she wrote this book she was a research fellow at the Oxford Centre for Management Studies, exploring the future of management education. Her other activities include helping disabled people find jobs in the computer industry, working on a seven-country study of people's attitudes and values about work, lecturing and career counseling in European business circles, learning about management in China, skiing, supporting local jazz groups, and maintaining an aging house in North London.